Ostrich

Ostrich

Edgar Williams

REAKTION BOOKS

For Karen and Laura

Published by
REAKTION BOOKS LTD
33 Great Sutton Street
London EC1V 0DX, UK
www.reaktionbooks.co.uk

First published 2013
Copyright © Edgar Williams 2013

Printed and bound in China by C&C Offset Printing Co., Ltd

British Library Cataloguing in Publication Data
Williams, Edgar Mark, 1960-
    Ostrich. – (Animal)
    1. Ostriches. 2. Ostrich products industry – History.
    I. Title II. Series
    598.5'24-DC23

ISBN 978 1 78023 039 9

Contents

Introduction

The ostrich is a bird everyone recognizes easily; not because it is brightly coloured, like the peacock or parrot, nor because it looks intelligent, like the owl, but rather for its sheer size and ungainly appearance. The ostrich is a unique bird; its large size excludes it from flying and it is strictly *terra firma*-bound. At nearly 3 metres tall and weighing up to 150 kg, it cannot climb trees to escape predators, so has undergone a series of remarkable adaptations that allow it to live and thrive in the open arid regions of Africa. Without the need to keep its mass low for flying, it has evolved long muscular legs. If danger approaches, it does not need to fly away: it can outrun its predators instead and delivers a lethal kick if cornered. Another consequence of losing the ability to fly is that the feathers of the ostrich only serve to protect it from the heat of the fierce midday sun. These unique and peculiarly fluffy feathers have attracted man's attention from early times. They were made into fans to cool the Pharaoh's brow in ancient Egypt and have provided a jaunty adornment to many a cap and cape. The continued demand for these feathers almost caused the extinction of the ostrich but in the end provided their ultimate protection. Like many other flightless birds – such as the dodo, great auk and moa – the ostrich could have been exterminated.

The ostrich belongs to an ancient group of flightless birds known as ratites, which dates back 80 million years, and which

are now found mainly in the southern hemisphere. They include the Australian emu, the South American rhea and the New Zealand kiwi. Although the ostrich is the largest of the present-day ratites, its recently extinct cousins were even larger. These flightless giant birds managed to colonize the isolated land masses of the southern continents. Just how they achieved this has intrigued ornithologists for centuries and is a puzzle that was solved only recently.

Since our early origins were in Africa, mankind has always existed alongside the ostrich. Some of the earliest artwork in existence has been found in South Africa, scratched on 60,000-year-old fragments of ostrich eggshell. The early cradle of civilization that stretched across Arabia, North Africa and later southern Europe was also the natural range of the ostrich,

ensuring its inclusion in the historical records, both written and illustrated.

An emu with her chicks, a close relative from Australia.

The meteoric demand for ostrich feathers in the fashion industry of the mid-nineteenth century led to a significant economic boom worldwide. History shows us that bust always follows boom and the changing world in the early twentieth century conspired to make ostrich and their feathers valueless. Many who had made their fortunes now lost them. Phoenix-like, the ostrich rose again as an economic force in the 1970s as the market for ostrich products – leather, meat and feathers – revived.

The ostrich's physical, metaphorical and metaphysical presence fills our written and collective memory. It is a bird known

The cassowary leads a solitary lifestyle in the jungles of Papua New Guinea and Northern Australia.

worldwide. Extracted from the arid peripheries of the African deserts, it is both mocked and celebrated, and transformed into abstract form in fine art and fiction. The ostrich, its feathers and its eggs are used as metaphors for justice and renewal; it can represent the chivalrous ideal or the ultimate in indecision.

1 Flightless Birds, Extinct and Extant

The origins of the ostrich and its flightless relatives are surprisingly complex and until recently were an enigma. It is only with modern genetic techniques that light has been shed on the subject. Because it is flightless, the ostrich's sternum (the bone supporting the ribs) lacks the normal ridge, called the keel, seen in other 'airborne' birds. In flying birds this important ridge provides the anchorage point for the extra-strong muscles required to flap the wings with sufficient power to fly. Taxonomists, by following this nautical analogy, thought that the keel-less ostrich sternum was more 'raft'-like, which when Latinized gives the word ratite. Nowadays these 'flat-chested' birds are only found scattered across the land masses of the southern hemisphere. The ostrich (genus *Struthi*, a single species) from Africa is the largest bird in the group, followed in turn by the emu (*Dromaius*, one species) in Australia, then the cassowary (*Casuarius*, three species) of New Guinea and northern Australia, the rhea (*Rhea*, two species) of South America and the much smaller kiwi (*Apteryx*, five species) of New Zealand. In addition there are some species of ratites that became extinct only recently, in the last 600 years or so, and were larger even than the ostrich: the moa (*Dinoris giganteus*; eleven species) from New Zealand and the elephant bird or roc (*Aepyornis*, three species) from Madagascar.

While the ostrich is currently the largest ratite in the world, it has had this title for less than 150 years. The Madagascan (Malagasy) elephant bird – the legendary roc of Arabian folklore – was the largest bird ever to have lived. Living on the remote island of Madagascar, with no natural predators, it became bigger and bigger, filling the ecological niche of the large mammalian herbivores and omnivores not present on the island. Successful for around 60 million years, it was only with the arrival of European explorers in the seventeenth century that it was completely wiped out in less than 200 years. Three metres tall and weighing around 450 kg, with a powerful neck, long muscular legs and sharp claws, it must have been a formidable creature, and could easily defend itself from sailors looking for an easy meal. However, its Achilles heel was its eggs: since it only laid one at a time, it was very vulnerable to predation. Like the bird, the eggs were huge: 90 cm in diameter and 30 cm long, with a capacity of 9 litres. In tropical climes these large eggs, once stolen, provided a good source of easily transportable fresh food, and the leftover shells could be used as drinking vessels or carved and decorated for sale. It went the same way as the dodo, its egg rather than its flesh providing food for hungry seamen. Another large extinct ratite is the giant moa (*Dinornis giganteus*) of New Zealand. Again, with no native predators the birds thrived for thousands of years until the arrival of the first Maori in the tenth century. By the time Europeans arrived in 1770, the giant moa had been hunted to extinction. Of the eleven species of moa, the smallest – the pygmy moa – was the last to become extinct, perhaps as late as the 1860s. Luckily the kiwi managed to survive in New Zealand, saved by its shy and nocturnal nature. The rhea and emu survived this period as their geographical range, like that of the ostrich, stretched inland from the coast to open semi-arid regions, so they were immune to passing sailors looking for fresh

An ostrich skeleton. The rudimentary wings and the flattened sternum supporting the ribs gives this group of birds their common name, ratite.

The extinct giant
moa (*Dinoris
giganteus*) of
New Zealand in
a watercolour by
Lord Rothschild,
1907.

food. One emu was not so lucky: a dwarf species found only on Kangaroo Island was killed off by visiting sailors and sealers and land clearance, and became extinct by 1830. Cassowaries, like the kiwi, still thrive because of their dense jungle habitat and their additional fierce temperament.

In the nineteenth century, when modern taxonomy began, the question of how to classify the ostrich caused quite a problem. Some thought it should be classified along with bats, as they were both not quite like typical birds. Others scientists placed the dodo (which some taxonomists even doubted had ever existed) with the ostrich; they shared the same grouping for a while because their beaks were grouped with those of hawks and parrots. Whole ostrich specimens were rare, and what made classification harder was the mixing up of emu, rhea (then known as the American ostrich) and cassowary parts. Other taxonomists were less sure and saw the ostrich and all flightless birds as a rag-bag of species, grouping the ratites with other flightless birds such as penguins and bustards. The biologist and palaeontologist Thomas Huxley (1825–1895) labelled them 'waifs and strays'.[1]

Huxley was one of the first scientists to posit the idea that birds were descended from dinosaurs, and that the ostrich was a direct descendant of the upright dinosaurs like the raptors, of which group *Tyrannosaurus rex* was a member. Huxley was a champion of Charles Darwin's new ideas of evolution. However, this direct link was challenged with the discovery in 1861 of the *Archaeopteryx*. This raven-sized fossil bird or feathered dinosaur was thought to represent a more likely link between dinosaurs and birds, and unlike the ostrich it was small and volant (able to fly).[2]

Charles Darwin (1809–1882), while making his famous circumnavigation of South America aboard the *Beagle*, made multiple observations of the rhea, and later used it along with the ostrich as example of the idea that natural selection or evolution was

An artist's impression of the extinct elephant bird (*Aepyornis*).

driven by use and disuse, in the case of the ostrich losing its wings through lack of use while enlarging its legs through increased use:

> The ostrich indeed inhabits continents, and is exposed to danger from which it cannot escape by flight, but it can defend itself, by kicking its enemies, as efficiently as many quadrupeds. We may believe that the progenitor of the

ostrich genus had habits like those of the bustard, and that, as the size and weight of its body were increased during successive generations, its legs were used more and its wings less, until they became incapable of flight.[3]

Huxley's view that the ostrich and other ratites had diverse origins was also championed by the naturalist Sir Richard Owen (1804–1892), who suggested that they shared many common features with other birds and that it was their 'arrested development of wings unfitting them for flight' that was the only common link between them.[4]

Over the next century, opinions were split between those who viewed the ratites as monophylic (sharing a single common ancestor) and those who thought they were polyphylic (with ancestors of various origins). By the end of the twentieth century, anatomical studies suggested a monophylic origin. However, this view presented a major geographical problem. How did the various ratites, being flightless, end up distributed around the southern hemisphere, separated by vast tracts of ocean, and why were they not found in the northern hemisphere? Fortunately the science of paleogeography came to the rescue. Their peculiar geographical distribution was explained by the ratites having a common ancestor that lived in Gondwana, a supercontinent occupying the southern hemisphere some 500 million years ago. The divergence of the ratites from this common ancestor would have started there during the mid-Jurassic period, about 170 million years ago, before Gondwana began slowly to break apart. It eventually formed today's southern land masses, first by breaking in two: one half contained Africa and South America, and the other half became Antarctica, Australia, New Zealand and Madagascar.

The ratites on these land masses eventually evolved into the birds we see today. This seems to provide a good explanation

Henry William Pickersgill (1782–1875), *Sir Richard Owen (1804–1892)*, 1844, oil on canvas. The British palaeontologist is shown holding the leg bone of a moa.

of why the ostrich is more similar to the American rhea than the geographically closer Malagasy elephant bird. However, this so-called 'vicariance biogeography' hypothesis failed to answer all the questions about ratite origins, particularly those raised by modern genetics. This hypothesis would suggest that those ratites that shared the same land mass should be the most related; hence the New Zealand kiwi and moa, since they were isolated from Australia for many millions of years, should be 'sister' species.

Comparing the genetic codes of the ratites finally proved that they were indeed descended from a common ancestor. To everyone's surprise, however, the moa and kiwi were revealed not to be 'sister' species. The kiwi is more closely related to the Australian emu instead, though they are separated by hundreds of miles of ocean.[5]

The reason for this conundrum is that their common ancestor of 80 million years ago was able to fly. The ratites evolved from this ancestor in a paraphylic (parallel) fashion, even sharing an ancestry path with the present-day tinamous, a South American bird that can fly.[6] The loss of flight occurred at various times in the past; for the ostrich it was around 70 million years ago. This ability of the ancestral ostrich to fly explains its current distribution both geographically and genetically. The early ancestor of the ostrich, *Palaeotis*, is known to have a Eurasian origin, as early fossil remains have been found in Eocene deposits (40 million years ago) in Eastern Europe. This then led to a later dispersal across modern Eurasia and Africa. Ostrich fossils do not appear in Africa until later on in the Miocene period (20 million years ago). If the ancestral ostrich was flightless and derived directly from Gondwana, the fossil record would be the other way around. While the theory of monophyletic vicariance is no longer believed, there are still some uncertainties as the ratite fossil record is incomplete. For instance, the lack of fossils in Antarctica does not support the notion that the Australasian ratites originated in South America.

Flightlessness allows birds to gain in size, and as there were no large predatory mammals such as big cats or wolves in Gondwana, the large flightless birds were able to successfully compete with smaller mammals, such as the marsupials common to

Australasia. In New Zealand, which has no indigenous mammals at all, they had no competition whatsoever. The ostrich gained its size advantage by living in semi-arid conditions and surviving better there than its mammalian predators. Its size allowed the ostrich to see its prey from further afield and to outrun its predators if chased. The increase in size also meant that the ostrich's egg became larger and stronger, which before man came along was another evolutionary factor that favoured a larger bird.

The fossil record of the ostrich and the other ratites shows that they form their own group, the Palaeognathae. All other living birds are grouped in Neognathae. The oldest ostrich fossil dates to 20 million years ago, from the Lower Miocene epoch, and was found in Namibia.[7] Fossil remains of the early ostrich (or *Struthio* genus) are fairly common and well documented, being found across Asia and Africa. *Struthio linxiaensis, S. wimani* and *S. mongolicus* were from China and Mongolia respectively, and *S. brachydactylus* and *S. orlovi* were from central Asia, while *S. coppensi* and *S. kakesiensis* were found in Namibia and Tanzania respectively. All these extinct species are based on finds of just bone fragments and eggshells. Indeed, *S. chersonensis* is named after a single large intact egg found in a riverbank in the late 1850s near Kherson, a Ukrainian city on the edge of the Black Sea. No one knows why none of these species survived. In China one species survived at least until the last Ice Age but became extinct soon afterwards.

By the beginning of the nineteenth century only two species of ostrich were thought to exist. By now their range had shrunk to just the lands around the Persian Gulf, the Middle East and Africa. One species, described as a dwarf ostrich and found in North Africa, was called Levaillant's ostrich (*S. bidactylus*) after the noted French ornithologist François Levalliant (1753–1824), who first described the bird.[8] No remains have ever been found

A print from 1874 showing the three largest ratites – the ostrich, cassowary and emu.

of it, so its very existence is in doubt. It is most likely a figment of the imagination of an overzealous ornithologist. It is very likely that at this time there was, as today, only one species of ostrich (*S. camelus*). It is only recently that its habitat became confined to Africa, for at the end of the Second World War a sub-species, the Arabian ostrich (*S. camelus syriacus*), was found widely across the Middle East. While plentiful in Georgian and Victorian times, its numbers declined rapidly and the last recorded sighting of a living specimen was made in the 1960s. It became extinct mainly because of over-hunting and ignorance of its endangered status.[9]

The remaining four sub-species are found on the savannahs of Africa, with the northern and southern birds separated by the vast equatorial rainforest belt of central Africa. They share a distribution with many herbivorous mammalian species such as the giraffe and the zebra. One sub-species, the southern ostrich (*S. camelus australis*), is found in the vast arid regions of Namibia, Botswana and South Africa. The common North African or red-necked ostrich (*S. camelus camelus*) is found widely across the arid regions of North Africa. Until recently its range stretched from the Atlantic Ocean in the west to the Red Sea in the east and it was abundant all along the Mediterranean coast from Morocco to Egypt. Now its range is restricted to a narrow band of sub-Saharan countries in West Africa. This is the largest of the sub-species, and as its name suggests it has a red neck (at least, the males do).

The Masai ostrich (*S. camelus massaicus*) is found in the mountainous regions of East Africa in a relatively small area overlapping Kenya, Tanzania, southern Ethiopia and south Somalia. It is unusual in having some feathers on its head and neck. It has pink skin on its thighs, which brightens in the male during the breeding season. The Somali ostrich (*S. camelus molybdophanes*) is found across the Horn of Africa, mainly in Somalia and Ethiopia. It differs from other ostrich in that it does not like the open plains but prefers the bush and scrubland. It is a browser rather than a grazer. Furthermore, rather than living in flocks, it prefers to be solitary or live in pairs. Its skin has a blue tinge which brightens with the breeding season, and the female's plumage is more brown than grey. This skin colouring has led to the common name of blue-necked ostrich. Recent genetic studies suggest that the Somali ostrich may be a separate species, since it has adapted to a different ecological niche with its own unique behaviour. Its geographical isolation has prevented hybridization with its neighbours to the north and west.[10] Such a reclassification would place the wild North African blue-necked ostrich on the endangered creatures list.

A male Masai ostrich (*Struthio camelus massaicus*).

The Somali ostrich (*Struthio camelus molybdophanes*), showing the silvery blue sheen of its skin.

Ostrich numbers were once huge, in the millions, but they are ever-declining in the wild. Why should this be, when the wild ostrich lives in such unpopulated arid regions of the African continent? It seems that in many places it is due to the process of desertification. Since the ostrich is herbivorous, it does need some vegetation to survive. Man's encroachment on the edges of these arid areas does not help; nor does over-grazing by domestic animals such as goats and cows. As we shall see later, the ostrich has been saved by man through domestication, as its feathers became an increasingly valuable commodity in the fashion houses of Europe and North America. Today farmed ostrich meat is becoming ever more popular, ironically providing the species – or at least a modern hybrid of the remaining African sub-species – with a guarantee of its future survival.

A good example of the gradual decline in the ostrich's distribution across its geographical range is its historical distribution in Egypt.[11] Eggshell fragments from Palaeolithic Egypt are found along the Nile Valley and rock art from this time illustrates ostrich being captured in traps. Throughout the Old, Middle and New Kingdoms (3000–1000 BC) the ostrich was still widespread and appears in many bas-reliefs and paintings. The bird continued to flourish during the conquests by Alexander the Great (332 BC) and the Romans (30 BC). The ostrich next appears in historical records in the fourteenth and fifteenth centuries, when it was still found widely across Egypt, but by the end of the sixteenth century it was only found in isolated pockets in the north around the Nile delta and on the coast around Alexandria, the Gulf of Suez and the Sinai Peninsula. Contemporary European travellers reported seeing large flocks of birds numbering 60 or more. The decline in numbers begins from the seventeenth century onwards, when the birds were still found along the Alexandrian and Red Sea coasts, but were spotted in much smaller numbers, often just singly. By 1850 the ostrich in the north was extinct and the only pockets of ostrich habitat left were in the Western desert bordering Sudan. The last sightings of a wild ostrich there were made in 1991. Sightings since then are thought to be of escapees from ostrich farms.

A pride of South African ostrich; the country is home to the world's largest population.

An aerial survey of wildlife made in 2010 by the Kenyan and Tanzanian wildlife services showed that the Masai ostrich was the sixth most common large animal out of 27 surveyed, with the zebra, Grant's gazelle, wildebeest, giraffe and eland being the most abundant. In the four areas surveyed (total area 24,371 sq. km) there were 1,461 ostrich, matching the number of elephants, giving a density of about one bird per 10 sq. km. Compared to a survey taken in 2007, the numbers had declined by 11 per cent, while the number of large mammals like elephants and giraffes had increased.[12]

In areas where commercial hunting is allowed, the ostrich has not done so well. In 2011 the Botswanan government banned ostrich hunting when a survey found that in the Okavango delta the ostrich population had declined by 95 per cent in fifteen years. The policy of promoting photographic safaris has now been adopted by the country instead. This foresighted policy may ensure the survival of the ostrich in the wild well into the twenty-first century and beyond.

2 Form, Function and Habitat

The ostrich is a remarkable creature. By losing the ability to fly, it has evolved to become the largest of birds and has developed many of the characteristics of the terrestrial quadrupeds with which it shares its environment. Its lifestyle and adaptation to an arid environment have allowed many unique qualities and attributes to develop.

The ostrich is heavy at 100–150 kg and tall at 2–3 metres high, with long muscular legs of around 1.5 metres in length and a distinctive swan-like neck of around 1 metre. Its body is shaped like a chicken's, and is about 1 metre long from front to back, with a downward-pointing tail. The wings are short and stubby; when extended, they are 1 metre each in length. They are nowhere near big enough to support flight, nor do they have enough muscular power for it. The flightless ostrich thus has to be fleet-footed to survive predation and find food. Removing the evolutionary pressures that flying imposes – the necessity of remaining light, aerodynamic and energetic – has given the ostrich an opportunity to exploit and adapt to the same environmental niches as herbivorous mammals.

The male bird's plumage is generally jet-black with long white feathers on its wings and tail. In females and juveniles the black is replaced by grey or brown, while newly hatched chicks are mottled brown, camouflaged like dried vegetation. During the

The female ostrich (above) is more drab-looking than her male counterpart (below).

The body feathers of a female ostrich.

day, ostrich are easily spotted, especially when living in flocks in open areas, but at night, when sitting down, they are perfectly camouflaged. There are no feathers on the bird's sides or thighs or under the wings. The neck and head are covered in short, spiky hair-like feathers that look more like fur. The skin is typically a greyish white colour, but in males it can be tinged red or blue during the breeding season depending on the sub-species. Over the body and legs the skin is wrinkled but it becomes more scaly and crocodilian on the lower legs.

Ostrich feathers are different to those of most birds. Instead of having flight-worthy rigidly barbed veins on either side of the shaft, they are – irrespective of body location – soft, downy and symmetrical in structure. The barbs are not linked together by minute hooks, as in most bird feathers. There are six types, which can be placed into three broad categories: soft downy ones, or floss, such as those found under the wings; plumes, such as those on the wing edge; and hard feathers, such as those on the wing surface.[1] Males typically produce more feathers than females. The feathers' main function is temperature regulation, while the long white feathers play a display role both in sexual selection, when males display to females, and during aggression between males. These feathers do not need to be preened, so ostrich lack a preen gland like those of flying birds. The fluffiness of these feathers, particularly the long white plume feathers of the male, has given the ostrich a unique place in history, as we shall see later.

The anatomy of the ostrich is not that dissimilar to that of any other bird. Its anatomy was minutely described in 1864 when at the Dublin Zoo a female died from a broken leg and a male froze to death on an unexpectedly cold night.[2] Autopsies were performed on the birds with great skill and even today these provide a useful anatomical guide. The main features noted were the well-developed gizzard, and a remarkable 14-metre-long intestine. The herbivorous ostrich eats large amounts of vegetation, so it requires a longer digestive system than other birds. This extra length allows for more efficient extraction of nutrients and fluid.

The ostrich's pelvis is different from that of other birds in that it is structured to allow the centre of gravity to remain between the legs. The long neck provides a counterbalance to the weight of both the extra-long gut and the gizzard. The ostrich has a neck of a most peculiar and unique structure. It is the longest neck of all birds; it is only surpassed in proportion by that of the giraffe. The neck's unusual structure allows the ostrich to keep its neck vertical and its head horizontal whether standing still or running at full speed. The obvious survival advantage of having a tall, upright neck is that it provides a good all-round view of any approaching predators and allows the bird to spot any juicy vegetation. The advantages do not stop there: its length, combined with the ostrich's modified pelvis and balanced centre of gravity, allows the bird to reach the ground without bending its legs.

The ostrich can turn its neck backwards through 180 degrees, allowing it to clean its feathers. It makes complex movements of its neck while it is feeding and mating and during defensive stances. The neck is relatively thin and featherless but is covered in fluff; in males the skin of the neck changes colour during the mating season. Inside the neck at the front is a rigid tube called the trachea, which is used for breathing, vocalization and temperature regulation. Behind this it is the gullet, a soft collapsible tube used for digesting food and water. These two tubes are supported by eighteen neck vertebrae, surrounded by muscle and joined together by tendons and two important ligaments. The unique arrangement of these structures allows the ostrich to perform the range of motions described above. The neck has four distinct regions: the head and upper region allows torsion while the lightest part of the neck, the cranial neck, allows the complex manoeuvres. The middle region allows forward and backward movement, and the so-called caudal region provides most of the supporting power.[3] Surprisingly, most of the scientific interest shown in how the ostrich's neck works is aimed at providing clues on how long-necked dinosaurs such as Diplodocus managed to carry their heads during feeding and locomotion.

The delicate neck is one of the bird's weak points. Many stories tell of how vulnerable the ostrich is to fatally breaking its neck, particularly when running through dense brush. One observer's

report illustrates this fact well: one day, while watching ostrich, he saw one get its head caught in the fork of a tree. In an attempt to free itself it jumped backwards, and ended up breaking its neck and decapitating itself.[4]

A cock during courtship displaying his wing feathers.

One consequence of a long flexible neck is that the weight of the head has to be kept to a minimum, as turning a bigger head would require bigger muscles and therefore a bigger neck. Long-necked dinosaurs faced a similar evolutionary conundrum. The ostrich head-to-body proportion is remarkably small, and the

The ostrich neck is an elaborate structure allowing the bird to remain vigilant at all times, even when eating.

Philippe de la Hire (1640–1718), *Dissection of an Ostrich's Neck*, black and red chalk.

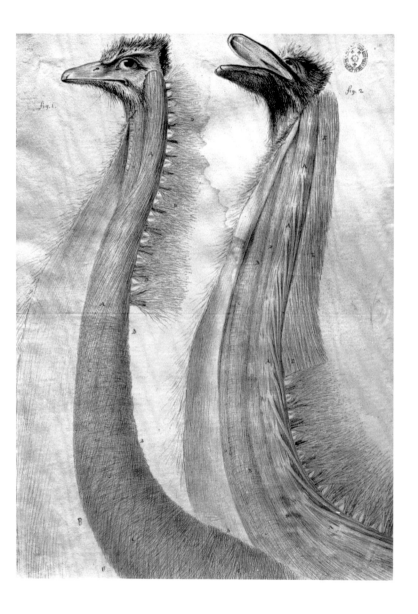

fig. 1.

fig. 2

brain inside is even smaller, weighing around 26 grams, or around 0.015 per cent of the whole body weight. This proportion is small in comparison to other birds, seventeen times smaller than a domestic chicken's brain-to-body ratio, for example.[5] The cranial bones are sponge-like, again reducing the head's weight. The ostrich's brain has little grey matter and a small olfactory centre, suggesting that the bird does not have a strong sense of smell or much intelligence.

This brain structure determines the way the ostrich sleeps. During deep sleep the ostrich, although stationary, keeps its eyes wide open. It can even remain standing with an upright neck. Only when its goes into REM sleep, equivalent to the dreaming state in humans, does it close its eyes. Its neck then begins to droop and sway before being jerked back upright. To an uninformed observer the bird looks as though it is struggling to keep awake, when in fact it is already asleep.[6] It is hard to say if the ostrich dreams, but its brain shows some similarities to mammals such as the duck-billed platypus, a primitive mammal, with an ancient lineage, that does not dream.

There is no doubt that ostrich have good eyesight matched with a strong sense of curiosity. One of the consequences of being the largest bird in the world is that the ostrich also has the largest avian eye. In fact, it has one of the largest eyes in the animal kingdom, at 5 cm in diameter. Some say the ostrich's eye is bigger than its brain. With good binocular all-round vision, it can easily detect any predators. The ostrich's eye is remarkably sophisticated and is especially adapted to view the horizon with enhanced acuity. It even possesses the ability for nocturnal vision.[7]

The ostrich is one of the few birds to have eyelashes. Unlike mammalian eyelashes, these are not hairs but short and curly rudimentary feathers without barbs which only cover the brow. The ostrich's beak is flat and broad and the tongue unremarkable, designed more for lubrication than taste.[8] There are no teeth, but the beak is quite dextrous and the ostrich is famed for its ability to pick things up, especially if they are shiny, and swallow them.

Their largely vegetarian diet reflects the flora in their environment and, not being fussy eaters, they have been known to eat insects and the occasional small lizard. Vegetation provides fluid, so ostrich can live in areas where surface water is scarce. The ostrich pecks at its food and stores it in its long expandable gullet as a large bolus. When large enough, the bolus is swallowed and passes into the gizzard, which is filled with stones of all sizes swallowed purposely by the bird. The roughly ridged gizzard and stones help to grind the vegetable material into a more digestible paste; it cannot digest inorganic material. Shiny objects are particularly attractive to ostrich, as anyone who has lost their wristwatch to one will tell you. It is this habit that has led to the myth that the bird eats iron for nutritional reasons. Although it lacks a bladder, the ostrich, unlike other birds, excretes its urine separately from its faeces as moist dung; this is a characteristic that is seen more commonly among animals than birds.[9]

Flightless birds need to be able to escape their predators quickly. The ostrich can run fast even from a young age. Adult birds have been observed running for 30 minutes at 60 km per

The ostrich ear.

hour (around 38 mph). As the ostrich is very good at getting around, it usually lives in large territories, the size of which depends on the abundance of vegetation; if the area is very arid, like the Namibrand desert in Namibia, the birds can daily range over 80 sq. km. In less arid regions, like East Africa, the range is as little as 10 sq. km.[10] Over its 60-year lifespan the ostrich will spend around eight hours a day on the move.

The legs of these birds are unique among the bird world; apart from being the longest, they are remarkably adapted for running and kicking. When running at full speed they have a stride length of 5 metres and they can easily crush a man's rib-cage with an appropriately aimed kick. Birds' knees work in the opposite direction to those of mammals, so the ostrich can only

The ostrich beak.

An ostrich foraging.

defend itself by kicking forwards and downwards – therefore an ostrich has to face its attacker to defend itself. Its main predators are lions, cheetahs and occasionally leopards, though to be effective the lions need to hunt in a pack, and a group of cheetahs needs to work together. When male ostrich fight they aim to kick their opponent's rigid sternum with blows sufficiently forceful that its opponent loses its balance and falls over backwards. Ostrich are also agile enough to be able to jump and swim.

Their legs are constructed so that most of the muscle mass is on the relatively short upper limb above the knee, and the longer lower limb is mainly bone. Overall this gives the legs greater strength and flexibility. The arrangement of muscles and tendons ensures that the leg movement keeps the bird balanced as it runs. The tendons are unique in that they are very elastic, giving the ostrich an extra spring in its step.[11] All these

factors together mean that the gait of the ostrich is extremely efficient: very important when you spend most of your time walking around in an arid environment.[12] Another unique feature of the ostrich is its feet: whereas all other birds have three or four toes, the ostrich has only two on each foot (having lost the first and second toes, when it first emerged as a separate species). The largest toe (the third toe in other birds), which faces forward, is tipped with a large claw, which gives a combined foot length of around 21 cm. The other toe (fourth toe) is angled outward and is much shorter; it acts as an outrigger and is important in maintaining balance.[13] The ostrich walks almost on tiptoe, again unlike all other birds. This mode of locomotion is thought to have evolved from the bipedal dinosaurs, and fossil tracks of running dinosaurs look similar to those made by running ostrich. The loss of two toes clearly confers an evolutionary advantage,

An ostrich chasing a rival off its territory.

The two-toed ostrich foot, with its sharp claw on the main toe.

as it has on horses, which have only one toe. Reducing the number of toes reduces the lower-limb muscle mass and thus enables faster running speeds.[14]

The feet are protected by thick fat pads which help give the toes good grip. The central claw, which is triangular in section, is curved downwards and ends in a sharp point. It can grow up to 10 cm long. This not only makes it a formidable weapon for slashing, but it provides extra grip when the ostrich is running at full speed, especially on sandy or hard surfaces.

The colour of the scales covering the feet can be light or dark brown. The thighs of the cock change colour depending on their breeding status and range from white through flesh-coloured pink to crimson. When not breeding or when nest sitting, the colour fades.

While small birds and animals can shelter from the hot midday sun, the ostrich, because of its size, has little choice but to endure the heat. To survive this hot and arid environment

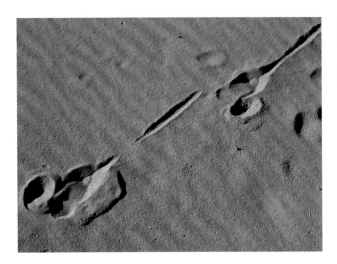

Ostrich footprints in the sand showing the impression of the two toes and the claws.

the ostrich has developed a number of special adaptations. Birds cannot sweat, so they have to regulate their body heat through the direct evaporation of water from their lungs. Ostrich eat plenty of succulent vegetation, which usually provides enough water for their needs. With ambient temperatures as high as 50°c, the birds keep their body temperature around 38°c.[15] Most birds have a higher temperature than this. Having a body temperature closer to that of mammals is a consequence of being flightless: the ability to fly requires a higher metabolic rate and thus a higher set body temperature. When ambient temperatures are lower than 38°c, the ostrich breathes slowly at between four and twelve breaths per minute, but when its surroundings get warmer, it begins to pant and the rate rises suddenly to a rapid 40–60 breaths per minute. In this way the ostrich can lose around 2 litres of water each day. If it becomes dehydrated, which is rare, its body temperature rises a few degrees and it takes bigger breaths. Two litres is the same amount a man would lose in his breath if exposed to the same environment, but he would double this amount by sweating. A dehydrated ostrich refuses food and seeks water, and can drink up to 10 litres of water in one go (a similar behaviour to the camel).[16] Prolonged panting creates its own problems, because if too much air is passed through the lungs it upsets the blood chemistry. The ostrich circumvents this problem via its own peculiar anatomy; its airway or trachea is structured so that when panting occurs the air is vented, purely by aerodynamic means, away from the gas-exchanging surfaces of the lungs. This means that only water evaporation can take place, which cools the bird without interfering with the gas exchange. The ostrich's lungs are thus perfectly adapted for their dual role of taking up oxygen and preventing overheating.[17]

Other cooling strategies are also used. The ostrich regulates 40 per cent of its heat loss through its beak, lower legs, feet and toes and its featherless neck.[18] When panting begins the ostrich will erect its feathers as well as spreading its wings and exposing its sparsely feathered regions. This may seem odd, as fluffing its feathers should enhance insulation, but instead of decreasing heat loss the behaviour acts to stop heat uptake from the hotter environment.[19] The largely featherless neck also plays a role in lowering temperature. Ostrich also cool themselves by standing into the wind and using their extended wings to direct air over their thighs and sides.[20]

Ostrich live in loose groups that usually consist of one cock and a dozen or so hens. The cock defends and patrols a territory of between 2 and 20 sq. km, and will chase off any male intruders. While defending his territory and during the breeding season, cocks make loud, low-frequency booming calls using their flexible and inflatable throats, which at these times is brightly coloured red or blue. The calls are remarkably loud and deep, containing more of the lower sound frequencies, as these frequencies increase the distance from which the call can be heard. Many say the sound is similar to a lion's roar. Early Victorian explorers often mistook ostrich calls for the roars of lions, especially when encamped at night, and were often disappointed, when out hunting, to find a lowly ostrich instead of a lion. The call is made while the beak is closed, with the sound being generated by air being forced back and forth between the lungs and flexible throat. Each call usually consists of two short booms followed by one long boom.

The cock will mate with more than one hen, and a major hen will form a loose partnership with the cock while tolerating several 'minor' hens. The hens range over a bigger area than the cock, as they require extra calories and nutrients during egg-laying periods. Breeding males display to females by squatting and showing off their white-feathered wings.

Both parents are equally involved in nurturing their offspring. The major hen creates a nest by scraping a hollow in the ground up to 3 metres in diameter. She then lays between five and twelve eggs over alternate days in the middle of the nest, while the minor hens lay eggs around the edges or, if there is no room, in the bush. If there are too many eggs in the nest, they cannot be incubated, and eventually the excess eggs roll out of the nest, never to hatch. The major hen seems to recognize her own eggs and ensures that they are always in the central core of eggs in the nest.[21] This is quite an achievement as the eggs look very similar.

The ostrich egg is the largest in the world, creamy in colour with a shiny surface pitted with pores of varying sizes, 15 cm in length, and 1.9 kg in weight. Ironically, in relation to the female's total weight they are among the smallest in the bird kingdom, representing less than 1 per cent of body weight. This egg-to-body-mass ratio means that the ostrich can lay many eggs without any great impact on its health. The fertile eggs in the nest are looked after only by the cock (or the most dominant cock when there is more than one in the group) and major hen. The eggs hatch within six weeks. The chicks are well looked after and reach sexual maturity at between two and four years old.

In one study, the average clutch size for each nest was 26–7 eggs. The peak in egg laying occurs at the beginning of the wet season. After the first rainfalls there is plenty of succulent vegetation available, which is important for the female ostrich and her future chicks. Predation of nests can be quite high, with 80 per cent of nests being abandoned or destroyed by predators. Single eggs, often laid in the bush, are less likely to be found and eaten, but still around 60 per cent are lost. If a female ostrich is ready to lay and there is no fresh nest to lay the egg in, she will lay her single egg alone away from the nest or in the nest of another male ostrich.[22] Investing time and energy in incubating eggs (communal in origin) is obviously something the dominant male and female ostrich have to negotiate; too large a brood is unmanageable and too small not worthwhile. This selective behaviour has given rise to the biblical parable of the female ostrich abandoning her young to fate.

The ostrich breeding system has been found to be more complex than it at first seems. Studies have shown that up to 70 per cent of the eggs in any one clutch were not from the resident territorial male or major hen and were related to the minor hens. To complicate matters further, the dominant male mated with ostrich outside his territory while the major hen laid eggs as a minor hen in surrounding nests. Communal nesting and monogamous parenting may seem at odds, but this behaviour has evolved to overcome the pressures of high egg predation that arise from having such large uncamouflaged eggs, and then to protect the hatched chicks by paying them close attention.[23]

A female ostrich tends her eggs.

The main predators of ostrich eggs are spotted hyenas, jackals, Egyptian vultures and lions. In daylight the bright white, shiny, unattended eggs are easy to see; in addition, the nests can be located by parental activity. From the air the eggs are also conspicuous and Egyptian vultures have been observed dropping stones on to the nests in order to crack open the eggs.[24] Fortunately, as the ostrich have such large territories their nests are sparsely distributed. One question is why the eggs are creamy white, as most birds that are ground nesters lay eggs that are pigmented and therefore better camouflaged. For ostrich the daytime temperature is more of an issue. Typically eggs are exposed to daytime temperatures over 30°c, so overheating is a threat to the developing embryo. Hatching success drops off above 40°c. While eggs with coloured shells would be more camouflaged, they would absorb more of the sun's radiation than the reflective white shells. Thus the ostrich has evolved a trade-off between losing eggs to predation or to overheating, which it has overcome by having a prodigious capacity for laying large, white eggs.[25]

After two weeks the parents take turns in incubating the eggs, which includes shading them when hot. The male and female take it in turns to sit on the eggs, each stint lasting for around eight hours. The hen starts in the morning, allowing the cock to browse for food. He browses in a haphazard way and finds the appropriate vegetation by serendipity, wandering from bush to bush, often covering great distances in the process. This form of random foraging allows the vegetation to recover. The hen feeds in the early morning and afternoon, so does not have the opportunity to wander as far, and will thus browse each plant she finds more thoroughly. At night the cock sleeps sitting on the nest while the female will sleep by the nest's side. While the unattended eggs are obvious, once sat upon by a parent, they become

An ostrich nest.

49

A hyena stealing an ostrich egg.

virtually invisible. When the hen is on the nest it crouches down. With its fleshy thighs covered by its wings and only its drab feathers exposed, it blends well into the surroundings, which are usually full of large stones, bushes and anthills. The darker cock is better camouflaged for sitting at dusk and night-time. This ability to lie flat on the ground led to the notion that the ostrich likes to bury its head in the sand. Ancient observers thought that the ostrich was assuming that it could not be seen with its head buried and that ignoring peril would make it disappear. The observation that the ostrich laid its eggs without incubating them right away also added to the notion that the birds were bad parents.

The birds, because of their weight, have to be careful when sitting down on the eggs, so they squat before lowering themselves on to the nest. While sitting on the eggs they maintain the nest by scraping soil and sand around the outer eggs. Slowly raising the floor of the nest in this way prevents flooding when the rainy season begins.

The chicks chirp inside their shells when ready to hatch and have to peck their way through. The parents do not seem to help, and are still keen to continue sitting on the eggs. After three to four days the parents abandon the nest and any chicks not yet hatched are left to die. The old and unfertilized eggs are broken and the contents eaten by the living birds. Again in the past this behaviour was misinterpreted, and it was thought that the cock was helping his chicks to hatch.

The cock will strongly defend the nest by hissing, chasing and kicking at any approaching predators. If they are close, he will just hiss, as kicking may lead to eggs being broken. Once they are hatched, the cock does not fight but protects the chicks by herding them to safety, leaving the hen to stand her ground. If the predator gets past the adults the chicks scatter in all directions and hide under vegetation, squatting motionless close to the ground. Sometimes the parents will try to distract the predator by feigning an injury, pretending to have a broken leg by limping or even falling over. Once the danger has passed the adults do not call out but use their keen eyesight to gather all the scattered chicks back together again. The chicks recognize their adult protectors and run back to join them. Being alone is deadly, as non-breeding adults and immature ostrich tend to peck at any solitary chicks, sometimes killing them.

When hatched, the chicks are already well developed, weighing on average a hefty 0.6 kg. They grow at a prodigious rate and within six months weigh around 60 kg. This 100-fold increase in mass is accompanied by a tenfold increase in height. As they grow, their limbs lose their yellow colour. They grow in

An ostrich chick.

proportion to the bird's height, giving young ostrich the same ability to run as adults.[26] Chicks from several nests, including the singletons hatched alone, are usually raised communally and protected by several birds. Despite this protection and their ability to hide in the vegetation, only 15 per cent of chicks survive their first year, by which time they are of adult size. These one-year-old immature birds exhibit a drab mixture of black and brown plumage. Early settlers in South Africa often mistook them for another species. At two years old the females can breed, while the males reach maturity after three to four years.

The ostrich has made the most of its dry environment. It survives in a quadruped's world: it can survive drought like the camel and the hot midday sun like the giraffe and can breed prolifically like the gnu. Its solutions to environmental stressors are not the same as those found in these mammals; it is purely avian, with the lengthened 'swan-like' neck, the enlarged 'eagle' eye, the exquisite 'peacock-like' fluffy feathers and the long 'turkey-like' legs. The ostrich has taken all these and more and become a tough bird with a long, long lineage stretching back to the dinosaurs.

3 Camel-bird

The ostrich has shared our cultural history from the beginning of the Stone Age, as recent excavations in the Diepkloof Rock Shelter at Western Cape, South Africa, show.[1] Pierre-Jean Texier from the University of Bordeaux and his team excavated the site and uncovered fragments of decorated ostrich eggshells dating back approximately 60,000–70,000 years. Scratched on to the fragments are repetitive patterns, lines and hatched band motifs. Dr Texier postulates that the decorations represent graphic communication and are symbolic representations allowing the individual and collective communication of identities, evidence of possible social and cultural exchange. Furthermore, the eggs have an open top, which strongly suggests that they were used as containers, most likely for carrying and storing water, a practice still in use today. Twenty thousand years later in Kenya, further finds of finely drilled ostrich-eggshell beads suggest that the bird had a cultural role in a society familiar with symbolism. These hunter-gathers most likely collected the eggs for food, as they provided a highly nutritious and protein-rich meal; it is doubtful that they were capable of catching the adult birds, as no sites have been found which contain butchered ostrich bones.[2]

Rock paintings and petroglyphs of ostrich are rarer than depictions of other African animals and birds, but do exist. In Namibia, at Twyfelfontein, a series of crude animal petroglyphs dating back

20,000 years survives. Among the depictions of giraffes and zebras, ostrich can also be found, sometimes alone and sometimes in groups.[3] A famous example of rock art is the so-called 'Blue Ostriches', which purportedly showed a group of five ostrich, two of which were painted with a bluish-grey hue, being approached by a San hunter disguised as an ostrich. Only copies of the artwork exist. The image was supposedly copied from a remote cave somewhere in South Africa by the respected artist G. W. Snow around 1867. Since the location of the cave, thought to be somewhere in the Wittebergen mountain range, is unknown and the original image has never been rediscovered, it is now believed to be a fake: a copy of a contemporary image from the book *Missionary Labours* (1842) by R. Moffat.[4]

The ostrich was well known across the ancient civilized world, and many writers gave detailed descriptions of it. Aristotle (384–322 BC) said of the Libyan ostrich:

> It has some of the characters of a bird, some of the characters of a quadruped. It differs from a quadruped in being feathered; and from a bird in being unable to soar aloft and in having feathers that resemble hair and are useless for flight. Again, it agrees with quadrupeds in having upper eyelashes, which are the more richly supplied with hairs because the parts about the head and the upper portion of the neck are bare; and it agrees with birds in being feathered in all the parts posterior to these. Further, it resembles a bird in being a biped, and a quadruped in having a cloven hoof; for it has hoofs and not toes. The explanation of these peculiarities is to be found in its bulk, which is that of a quadruped rather than that of a bird. For, speaking generally, a bird must necessarily be of very small size. For a body of heavy bulk can with difficulty be raised into the air.[5]

Decorated ostrich
eggshell fragments
from the early
Stone Age.

0   3 cm

To the ancient Greeks and Arabs the ostrich provided evidence
of a hierarchical link between the flora and fauna surrounding
them. They believed that there was a gradual transition from the
simplest insects and other animals through to man. This early
view of evolution cast the ostrich as the link between bird and

Prehistoric rock art of an ostrich, Wadi Auis, Libya.

four-legged beast. To the early Greek and Roman writers Xeno-phon (430–354 BC), Diodorus Silicus (60–30 BC), Strabo (64 BC–AD 24) and Pliny the Elder (AD 23–79), the ostrich was the στρουθο-καμήλος, or *Strouthokamilos* (camel-bird). Although it was very big, it was clearly a bird, with the obviously avian features of having two legs and feathers, but its other characteristics were similar to that of the camel. The Arabian and Northern ostrich also shared its geographical domain with the camel, both thriving in arid areas. The two-toed ostrich was thought to have a cloven hoof like that of the camel, which would allow it to walk on soft sand. Like the camel, it has a herbivorous diet and can go without water, and it was believed that the ostrich was able to retain water as the camel does. Other similar features are their eyelashes and long, bare necks.

Over the centuries, many described the ostrich's great size and its resemblance to the camel, its herbivorous diet and its liking for grain. It was sometimes thought that the ostrich, when running with outstretched wings, was actually flying, if only at ground level; its habit of swallowing things it shouldn't gave it the reputation of eating iron, flesh and fire.

The ancient Romans called it *struthiocamelus* (camel-bird); again half-bird, half-beast. This pre-Darwinian view was finally immortalized in the eighteenth century by the Danish botanist and taxonomist Carl Linnaeus (1707–1778), who while classifying the world of avifauna gave the ostrich its modern scientific name of *Struthio camelus* – literally bird-camel or sparrow-camel – mindful that the ostrich was the link between birds and mammals. The naming connection between the ostrich and sparrow is lost in the mists of the time and is probably a mistranslation from its Arabic name, of which no record survives. However, it is from this route that the ostrich derives its many vulgar names in today's modern languages, such as *strutsi* in Finnish, *strauss* in German, *struts* in Swedish, *avestruz* in Spanish and Portuguese and *struisvogel* in Dutch. The French *austruche* provides the route to the English noun 'ostrich'.

Archaeological evidence found in the Xinjang province of China shows that there was once an Asian species of ostrich

(*Struthio asiaticus*), which became extinct after the last ice age. Images of the bird, which was smaller than its modern cousins, can be found on prehistoric pottery and in cave drawings. After this time the only archaeological remains found are those of the Arabian ostrich; these show that its range may have extended into Central Asia during the Stone Age. Eventually it became extinct in this area too.

The first written Chinese records of the ostrich date back to the times when expeditionary and trading links with Persia were being established. General Chang K'ien (138–126 BC), reporting back to Emporer Wu-ti, remarked on the 'great birds with eggs of the size of pottery jars'. By AD 101 the Persians were sending ostrich and lions to China as diplomatic gifts. The Chinese initially called them *ta-ma-tsio* or 'bird of the great horse', then the 'Arsak' or Persian bird, and finally adopted the Arabian, Greek and Persian convention of 'camel-bird'.[6]

From AD 650 onwards live birds were transported along the Silk Road. How this was achieved, and what the rate of attrition, was never recorded. The birds that did make it were well looked after and ended up in the Emperor's menageries. Stone carvings of these birds can still be found on the slabs that line the tombs of Emperor Kao Tsung and Emperor Jui Tsang from the Tang period. These carvings are not only life-sized but clearly copied from life, unlike contemporary images from Europe.[7] The ostrich next appears during the resurgence of Chinese overseas missions, particularly to East Africa and the Arabian Peninsula, in the fifteenth century. This time the ostrich was named the 'camel crane', and its eggs were described as being as big as coconuts.

Unlike the rest of the world, the Chinese were enthralled by the ostrich for 800 years. They saw the ostrich as a zoological curiosity, and attached no special value to its extravagant feathers,

which is odd, since they used pheasant and peacock feathers widely in their decorative art.

The Persians were clearly not so enchanted by the ostrich as they were by birds such as the peacock. There are only a few fragments of artwork surviving from pre-Christian times.[8] Several cylinder seals have been found that show scenes from this region featuring the ostrich, dating back from the tenth to seventh centuries BC. These drilled-out cylinders were rolled over molten wax to leave a raised design. In one, measuring just 3 cm by 1.4 cm, a detailed hunting scene is depicted: a central character holds two adult ostrich by the neck which in turn are trying to kick their captor, while in the background several ostrich chicks can be seen, one in pursuit of a gazelle.

Ancient Egypt was surrounded by lands containing the ostrich, from the Arabian Peninsula to East Africa (Nubia, Ethiopia and Punt) and across North Africa. The Egyptian influence permeated all of these regions through trading and diplomatic contacts,

60

and there is plenty of evidence to show that this trade included the import and export of ostrich, ostrich feathers and eggs. In the rock temple of Abu Simbel are scenes illustrating a war between Ramses II and the Libyans and Nubians which show Ramses receiving tributes, including ostrich, from the Nubians. Another scene shows a captive ostrich being led, followed by a man with three ostrich feathers and a basket containing ostrich eggs. Whether these were whole eggs for eating or eggshells for decoration is unclear. The Egyptians likely had their own indigenous population of ostrich, particularly along the Mediterranean, Nile Delta and Red Sea coasts, and scenes showing ostrich and bustard hunting exist, including one famous example on the reverse of a gold ostrich-feather fan found in the tomb of Tutankhamen.[9] Whole eggshells were used for decoration and have been found in many tombs.

Ostrich plumes were worn by Egyptian soldiers to decorate their helmets. Unlike those of other birds, ostrich feathers are symmetrical along the shaft. The Egyptians took this symmetry to symbolize fairness, and they created a feather hieroglyph which was used at the time of the later Kingdoms to symbolize truth and justice. Ma'at, the goddess of cosmic order, truth, justice and righteousness, is often depicted wearing an ostrich-plume headdress. She keeps her eyes closed, much like the blindfolded Western figure of Justice. It was thought that the world would not function without Ma'at and her hieroglyph is included on many statues as a symbol of justice. The Greek historian Diodorus Siculus (90–21 BC) informs us that Egyptian judges wore small figures of Ma'at as the insignia of their office. This symbolism extended even into the afterlife: as described in the Book of the Dead, it was against Ma'at, symbolized as an ostrich feather, that the heart was weighed to ascertain its owner's worthiness to enter heaven.

Unguent box with a double royal cartouche form the tomb of Tutankhamen (*r. c.* 1361–1352 BC). The top is decorated with four ostrich feathers.

Biblical references to the ostrich are confined to the Old Testament, although the bird would still have been found living wild in the era of the New Testament. In Job 39:13–19 the ostrich is not depicted in a positive light, but is described as being imprudent, cruel, wild and uncouth:

> The wings of the ostrich wave proudly,
> But are her wings and pinions like the kindly stork's?
> For she leaves her eggs on the ground,
> And warms them in the dust;
> She forgets that a foot may crush them,
> Or that a wild beast may break them.
> She treats her young harshly, as though they were not hers;
> Her labour is in vain, without concern
> Because God deprived her of wisdom,
> And did not endow her with understanding.
> When she lifts herself on high,
> She scorns the horse and its rider.

Gold Egyptian pendant showing Ma'at with an ostrich-feather headdress.

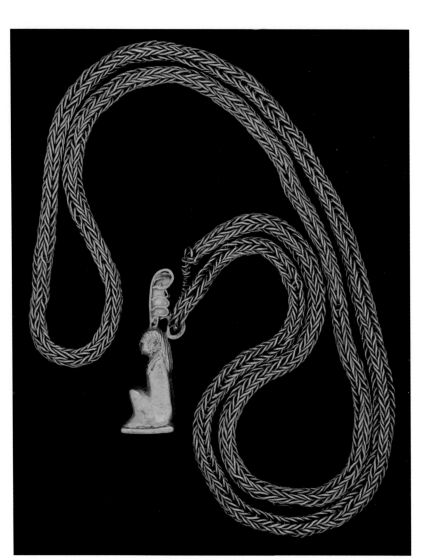

In the Lamentations of Jeremiah (4:3) the ostrich is used to illustrate the cruel behaviour of the Jews in times of crisis: 'Even jackals offer their breasts to nurse their young, but my people have become heartless, like ostrich in the desert.'

The ancient Romans would have been familiar with the ostrich, since large parts of Rome's southern empire overlapped with the habitat of the Arabian and northern ostrich. Like most large animals, the ostrich was used in public parades, and was often ridden like a horse, and even used to pull ladies' carts. In addition, it was enjoyed roasted at banquets. In 48 BC Julius Caesar, at the height of his powers after defeating Pompey and returning from a successful military campaign in the Middle East and Egypt, organized in Rome a series of triumphal parades. These not only included the spoils of his conquests but animals from the lands he had fought in, including elephants, big cats, a single giraffe, flamingos and ostrich.[10] In AD 281, during a venation (in which animals were slaughtered in the arena for entertainment) celebrating the victories of Emperor Probus, 1,000 ostrich, stags and boars, along with deer and sheep, were released into the Circus Maximus. The circus had been planted with many trees to make it look like a forest, and the general public were allowed in to slaughter as many beasts as they could. The ancient scriptures do not report the outcome of this mass slaughter, nor if the ostrich outran the plebeian participants.

Through the Dark Ages in Europe the ostrich briefly disappeared from recorded history, with the exception of the ostrich plume, which still adorned the headgear of military leaders. With the development of chivalry, the plume becomes a potent heraldic symbol and badge of authority, especially among the newly created knights of northern Europe. The ostrich plume, both black and white, was incorporated into many coats of arms. One of the most famous of these belongs to the Prince of Wales, whose

An early
18th-century
gold cameo
showing in onyx
the Prince of
Wales's feathers.

triple-plumed badge can to this day be seen across much of
Wales and England. This badge dates back to Edward of Wood-
stock (1330–1376), the eldest son of King Edward III, who is also
known as the Black Prince because he liked to wear black armour.
It is not known when he adopted the plume, but some stories
state that it was after he took the ostrich-plumed helmet from
the defeated King John I of Bohemia as he lay dead on the battle-
field at Crécy in 1346. However, it is much more likely that he
inherited it from his mother, Philippa of Hainault, whose family
may already have had the ostrich emblem in their arms. At first
only a single white plume was shown, but this later developed
into the triple plumes we see today, most notably on the front of
the current UK two-pence coin.

This theme has been extended to the logo of the Duchy of
Cornwall, the territory and land traditionally inherited by the
incumbent Prince of Wales. The logo shows two Cornish coughs,
each holding an ostrich feather, on either side of the Duke of
Cornwall's arms. The ostrich plume is included in many civic

•A gold coin from 1363–72 showing Prince Edward surrounded by four ostrich feathers.

Ostrich feathers have a long and continuing history on English coinage, as can be seen from the original design for the two-pence coin showing the triple ostrich-feather plume of the Prince of Wales.

Coat of arms of Charles de l'Aubespine (1580–1653).

coats of arms across England and Wales, and the number of plumes shown is between one and five, ranging in colours from white, silver and blue. In the arms for West Dorset the plume is shown as a quill in honour of the writer Thomas Hardy. Further examples can be found in the Welsh Rugby Union and Wrexham Football Club badges. The triple-feather plume was not exclusive to the Prince of Wales: on the European continent it was readily adopted by the senior military in the French Republic and soon became a badge of the ruling society.

The appearance of the ostrich itself is less common. Since it was thought at the time to symbolize faith and contemplation, it is found in a few armorial and family crests. A good example is the coat of arms of the French diplomat Charles de l'Aubespine,

Three ornate
ostrich-egg cups
with hinged lids,
from Dresden,
Germany, *c.* 1600.

which shows two ostrich holding a crowned shield displaying
panels decorated with the orders of St Michel and St Esprit. In
other examples the ostrich is shown with a metal object, such as
a horseshoe, in its mouth or claws, illustrating the belief that the

One in a series of drawings by the Dutch artist Peiter van Laer (1613–1673). This highly stylized ostrich is shown swallowing an iron nail and holding a horse-shoe in its claw.

bird could eat and digest iron. The Austrian city of Leoben, a steel-making town, exhibits in its coat of arms an ostrich that holds not one but two horseshoes.

Strangely enough, although their feathers were used through-out medieval Europe, few illustrations survive of the ostrich itself; those that are known appear in illustrated manuscripts and show little resemblance to the bird. One of the earliest images of the bird can be found in the Bayeux Tapestry. Completed in 1070, this embroidered cloth is famous for showing the Norman

The Bayeux Tapestry, the lower border showing an assida (ostrich) with the star Virgilia.

Conquest of England and more specifically the Battle of Hastings, during which King Harold was killed, supposedly by being shot in the eye with an arrow. While the central panels tell the story of the Conquest, the upper and lower borders are decorated with birds and animals. In a single panel depicting mounted cavalry, two ostrich are shown at the bottom edge.[11] Though they more closely resemble turkeys, they have long necks and are shown looking at the ground. The identifying factor is that the birds are accompanied by a star. At this time it was thought the birds did not lay their eggs until the star Virgilia appeared in the Pleiades constellation and rose in the June night sky. The embroiderers were evidently more familiar with this parable than with the bird itself.[12]

At this time the ostrich was known as Assida (camel-footed), and it appears in a few bestiaries of the time. The best known is the illustrated twelfth-century Aberdeen Bestiary, which contains a long sermon on hypocrisy in man using the characteristics of the bird as described in Job. The manuscript contains an illustration of two ostrich with three eggs. Though the birds depicted look more like eagles, they have the cloven hoofs of camel. One bird attends the eggs while the other is shown looking into the sky at the star Virgilia. The undersized eggs are shown resting on the ground and not in a nest, illustrating the belief that they were abandoned by the hen once laid. Two other bestiaries of the time show ostrich as having a bird's body with camel-like legs and hooves and a mammalian head with vulpine ears. Clearly the artists were guessing at the ostrich's appearance; the only information they had to work upon was its Latinized name – camel-bird – and that it was flightless, as the Bible states. Nowhere does the Bible mention its extra-large size or unusually long neck and legs.

The magnificent Sherborne Missal, a religious liturgical manuscript from the fifteenth century, is richly decorated throughout with 36 species of birds. While indigenous northern European species are accurately represented by the artist, there is also – amazingly enough – a small image of an ostrich, depicted standing next to two men and two hunting dogs. This rather crude depiction is important because it shows the ostrich accurately for the first time in European illustration; also, its inclusion in a hunting scene seems to suggest that the illustrator knew about the Arabian origins of this bird. It is unlikely that the illustrator drew the bird from life. They are more likely to have used a copy book sourced from southern Europe.[13]

The revolution in printing begun by Johann Gutenberg (1398–1468) meant that books could now be reproduced in their hundreds. It was at this time that the task of illustrating and cataloguing all of 'God's creatures' was begun. One of the first of these early taxonomists was Albrecht Dürer (1471–1528), who produced a series of woodcut prints of animals and birds. His image of the ostrich, while true to life, seems rather grotesque and ill-proportioned to the modern eye. Other early engraved images of the ostrich were depicted in more natural proportions as we would expect to see nowadays. The great Swiss naturalist Conrad Gesner (1516–1565) included a woodcut image in his great work *Historiae animalium* which to the modern eye obviously depicts an ostrich, though it is not quite accurate enough to have been drawn from life. In many ways it is anatomically incorrect: its head looks more like an eagle's, its two-toed feet are

ill-proportioned and its plumage is clearly guessed at. Gesner's ostrich is covered in the large decorative wing feathers that were used to decorate hats. Gesner admitted that he had never seen an ostrich: 'Some say that the bill should be broader . . . and that the feet should be cloven, as in calves . . . Let the eye-witness be the judge, for I have never seen this bird for myself.'[14]

Contemporary with Gesner was the Italian naturalist Ulisse Aldrovandi (1522–1605). His *Ornithologiae* contains an illustration of a pair of ostrich. Unlike Gesner's illustrations these images are more likely to have been drawn from life, as they are shown with more realistic plumage – the cock black on its body with its more showy plumage on its wings and tail, and the hen drab and slightly smaller. Included in the hen's image is an egg. Oddly the cock holds a bone in its beak while the hen holds a horseshoe.

In Tudor times little was known about the ostrich, or estridge as it was then called, except as a source of plumes. Ostrich plumes were still relatively rare and since they were expensive they represented authority and were largely worn by men. Several portraits of Henry VIII show him sporting a neat white ostrich plume in his cap; not erect, as became fashionable later, but lying horizontally across his forehead. While women in the Middle East

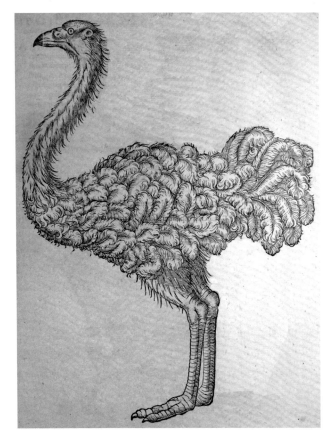

Ostrich from
Conrad Gesner's
Historiae animalium,
(1551–8).

decorated their clothes with feathers at this time, few Western women did so. However, a portrait of Katherine Parr painted in 1545, just after she became Henry VIII's sixth wife, shows her wearing a rich scarlet damask gown with a beaded headdress adorned with a small white ostrich feather. The purpose of this portrait is to portray her as Queen Regent, not just as the king's wife. Important Tudor aristocrats, keen to display their status, also wore ostrich feathers in their caps, but these were black rather than white. After the time of Henry VIII the ostrich-feather fan became fashionable, particularly in the last years of the reign of Elizabeth I (1533–1603), who was particularly fond of them. In three of a series of six portraits by John Bettes the Younger painted between 1585 and 1590 the queen is shown holding a large, sumptuous, bejewelled ostrich-feather fan.[15]

Rudolf II (1552–1612), the Holy Roman Emperor and king of Hungary and Bohemia, was pivotal in maintaining peace between European Protestants and Catholics. However, as he grew older he became more reclusive, and in his castle in Prague he became a great collector. His botanical garden and menagerie were considered wonders of their time, and were stocked with flora and fauna from across the known world. His exotic bird collection included Europe's first living dodo and two ostrich, which had been transported from Venice in 1603. The 335-mile journey took four days and was not easy either for the birds or their four attendants. The first stage, to Innsbruck, was undertaken by cart through rough mountainous terrain; after this they travelled by boat to Linz, followed by yet another overland haul and a final boat ride to Prague. The whole journey was a public spectacle, which added more stress for the ostrich. They survived the journey, but unfortunately were dead by 1607. The cause was probably malnutrition, as little was known about their long-term dietary requirements. Malnourished ostrich are prone to infection. The birds were not wasted, as Rudolf added them to his collection of mounted animal skins and skeletons.[16] Sadly as Rudolf aged his mental health declined and his collections were broken up.

The physician and author Sir Thomas Browne (1605–1682), famous for his book on religious tolerance and self-expression, *Religio medici*, also kept notebooks of short miscellania, which he published in 1646 as *Enquiries Into Very Many Received Tenents, and Commonly Presumed Truths*. These are now more commonly

John Bettes the Younger, *Elizabeth I* with ostrich-feather fan, c. 1585–90.

known as *Browne's Vulgar Errors*. One of Browne's enquiries concerned the ostrich and its ability to 'digesteth Iron'. His detailed discourse, titled 'Of the Ostrich', describes how the ancients confirmed the ostrich's habit of eating iron and stones to aid the mechanical grinding of its food. He then discusses whether the iron undergoes chemical corrosion, or 'chilification', as he terms digestion. Quite rightly, he concludes that any changes seen in the iron recovered from an ostrich's digestive system are due to chemical and mechanical corrosion alone and not the processes of digestion.

In 1660 two young Englishmen – John Ray, a clergyman and naturalist, and Francis Willughby, an aristocrat – met at the University of Cambridge. They were both naturalists and had a shared interest in ornithology, and decided to compile a scientific treatise on birds together. The contents were to be collected as they travelled around Europe for three years between 1663 and 1666, funded by Willughby. Unfortunately Willughby died of pleurisy in 1672 before the work was finished, but Ray finally completed and published it as *Willughby's Ornithologiae libri tres* in 1676. The work contains a plate illustrating the ostrich and its egg, sharing the page with a cassowary. Again, at first glance the image is easily recognizable as an ostrich, but on closer examination it seems to be made up of an admixture of parts. While the torso and plumage are correct, the head is similar to that of the cassowary, while the feet look three-toed. The juxtaposition of the two ratites on the same page seems natural to a modern observer, but for a seventeenth-century naturalist this was quite a revolutionary observation.

By the eighteenth century prints were hand-coloured, and a notable English book, *A Natural History of Birds* (1731–8) by Eleazar Albin, shows an ostrich that was most likely drawn from

The Ostrich, print of 1829.

a mounted (stuffed) museum specimen. The ostrich looks anatomically correct, but its plumage is poorly represented due to the simple colouring technique. George-Louis Leclerc, Comte de Buffon, the renowned French naturalist famous for his 36-volume catalogue of the animal kingdom, *Histoire naturelle* (1749–88), finally provided a realistic illustration of the ostrich along with a lengthy description of its anatomy.

Eighteenth-century descriptions of the ostrich resemble those of today. A pamphlet from 1741 correctly states that the bird voids any inedible objects it eats. The description of the eggs is accurate – they are described as being the size of a child's head – although the hen is still said to abandon her eggs after laying them in the sand. A new observation is that ostrich do not like pregnant women and will attack and kick anyone who is with child. This does not seem to be true: at least, there are no recorded cases of this happening in recent times. The idea of the ostrich hiding its head when in danger reappears around now, 'the Bird

An ostrich from Pierre Belon, *L'Histoire de la nature des oiseaux* (1555).

being so simple that when it hides its head in a bush it thinks
that its whole body is hid'.[17]

By the eighteenth century there were captive ostrich in the
UK; this could be achieved because they thrive in the European

The Ostrich, from Georges-Louis Leclerc, Comte de Buffon, *Histoire naturelle* (1801).

climate and are easy to feed. Ostrich were on public display in the Royal Aviary in St James's Park, London, at this time.

It was not until the nineteenth century that the Southern ostrich appeared in Europe. Some of the first ostrich from South Africa were collected from the Cape of Good Hope in 1804 by a French scientific expedition returning from Australia. Madame Josephine Bonaparte, the first Empress of the French, took delivery of three Southern ostrich to add to her collection of animals and birds at her country residence, Malmaison. Another arrived in 1808, along with some dwarf emus from Kangaroo Island, which were soon to become extinct.[18] At its peak Empress Josephine's collection was famed across Europe and attracted many visitors, both royal and republican. The collection flourished for a few halcyon years but declined rapidly after she was forced to divorce Napoleon Bonaparte in 1810 because she had been unable to bear him a child. After this she could no longer afford to maintain her animal collection and received no further state-funded

Ostrich, William Daniell, *Interesting Selections from Animated Nature* (1809).

imports from overseas expeditions. She died in 1814, after which
the remainder of her collection was sold off. What became of the
ostrich is not recorded, but it is likely that they ended up as
museum specimens, like those of Rudolf II.

In 1834 the Dublin Zoological Gardens at Phoenix Park contained at least one pair of ostrich. An article about them in the

William Cornwallis
Harris, *Ostrich*,
1840.

Dublin Penny Journal describes their voracious appetites, stating
that they would eat anything to hand, 'leather, grass, hair, iron,
stones or anything that is given'. It does go on to say that the
iron, glass and stones are not digested. The article continues by
describing the breeding habits of the ostrich and ends with a
paragraph on their plumes, telling how the ladies of the East
ornament their dresses with them, and how 'our undertakers
and our fine gentlemen . . . make use of them to decorate their
hearses and their hats'.[19] (This was before the time of the great
feather bonanza, when the feathers were plucked rather than
pruned.) At this time the inventory of London Zoo lists an
ostrich shed and yard containing four ostrich: three males from
Tripoli and a female donated by the Marchioness of London-
derry after its mate had died.[20]

By the beginning of the nineteenth century most large zoos
worldwide had ostrich on display, as the Northern and Arabian
ostrich were still common and easy to obtain and breed. Apart

from its general biology and associated myths, this large, flightless, rather gawky-looking bird served mainly as a curiosity. This was about to change as the Georgian period ended and the great Victorian age began. With the industrialization of the fashion industry, and the colonization of Africa, there were increasingly greater sums of money to be made from ostrich feathers as demand constantly outstripped supply. During this century more was written about the ostrich then ever before or since. How this demand led to great fortunes and ultimately to the domestication and commercial exploitation of the ostrich is told in the next chapter.

4 Ostrich *à la Mode*

The road that led to man's commercial exploitation of the ostrich first began in the wild. Its large egg contained a valuable source of protein, and once empty the eggshells provided material for making drinking vessels, bowls, storage jars and religious artefacts. Its feathers were worn by the military and royalty. It was the industrialization of fashion that catapulted the ostrich to being one of nature's most valuable assets, at one time earning more money for South Africa than gold. It was not the ostrich's egg but its feathers that led ultimately to its domestication.

The steady demand for ostrich feathers from the fourteenth century onwards was met by Arab traders supplying Europe and Asia. Feathers came from North and East Africa, with camel trains from sub-Saharan West Africa transporting the plumes across the desert to the great Mediterranean ports such as Alexandria. The male ostrich produces on its rudimentary wings the finest white plumes: these are the wing primaries. The best feathers were judged for their width and length, the floss of their willowy barbs, and their colour, 'white as milk and immaculate as new snow'. Wing coverts, which protect the white primary feathers, provide the shorter black feathers. The tail feathers were also used, but were not so prized.

In the fourteenth century ostrich feathers were worn in conical caps during the reigns of Edward III and Richard II. They

A Turkish ceremonial costume worn by a Colonel of the Janissaries, including a hat with a large ostrich feather aigrette, *c.* 1790.

were adopted by the military around the reign of Henry V. It wasn't until Tudor times that feather-wearing became fashionable among the ladies and men of the court. The flamboyant use of the ostrich feather as a fashionable millinery adornment was popularized in the UK by Georgiana Cavendish, née Spencer, Duchess of Devonshire (1757–1806), and in France by Marie Antoinette (1755–1793). Georgiana started by attaching ostrich feathers to her hair in an arc but soon went on to add more and more feathers to create more elaborate displays.[1] Thus began a millinery race among the leading ladies of fashion, with headpieces eventually becoming unmanageably and ludicrously large. The best plumes were both expensive and exclusive, two factors that ensure the success of any fashion item or trend. While the nobility were keen to follow this fashion, the general public saw the wearing of ostrich plumes as excessive. Wearing plumes was frowned upon so much that Queen Charlotte (1744–1818), wife of George III, eventually banned it at court. Nevertheless, over the next 150 years the demand for ostrich feathers grew exponentially; at its peak it required the production of millions of feathers.

Like all birds, ostrich moult, so in the early days, when demand was relatively low, this was an ample, simple and safe source of feathers. A disadvantage, however, was that the feathers were not all of good quality and had often been damaged through general wear and tear. By the mid-nineteenth century the Northern and sub-Saharan African ostrich had begun to be killed for their skins (leather) and feathers. The birds with the best plumes were killed and their skins, feathers still attached, were transported across the desert by camel to the southern Mediterranean ports. These trans-Saharan caravan routes linked Kano in Nigeria to Tripoli in Libya, Timbuktu to Essaouria (Mogador) on the Atlantic coast and Khartoum and Wadai to Benghazi,

Marie Antoinette with feathered headpiece, 1775.

overleaf:
left:
The Feather'd Hair in Flight, mezzotint on paper, 1777, after John Collett.

right:
The Preposterous Head Dress, lampoon of the feather fashion, 1776.

Libya (Sahara and Sahel) in the east. In Algeria and Morocco the feathers were plucked from the skins, which were then made into leather. Cleaning and processing the feathers was a particularly dusty and dirty job, and was performed by the lowest-paid workers, who suffered respiratory diseases as a consequence. From these ports the feathers were shipped across the Mediterranean to Marseilles in France and Livorno, Venice and Trieste in Italy.

As demand grew, wild ostrich numbers began to fall. Since killing the birds for their plumes was clearly unsustainable, feathers began to be plucked from living birds instead. Catching the wild bird alive was difficult, but at least they were free to breed after their release. Unfortunately for the ostrich, plucking was painful. It often damaged the follicles from which the feathers grew, which meant that only stunted feathers would regrow; the ostrich was left looking like a giant plucked chicken with its pink skin showing through.[2] A natural progression from this technique was ostrich ranching: corralling the wild ostrich after collecting eggs from nests in the wild. This technique was pioneered by local Arab potentates but soon became an attractive production method among pioneering European colonists who were trying their hands at making a bit of money. It did not require a great investment of capital, and there was plenty of

Ostrich farming in Toliara, Madagascar, from *Le Petit Journal* (21 February 1909).

A black wing feather, often woven into the turbans of young Wodaabe men during the Yaake dances, Niger.

arid land available for purchase that was unsuitable for conventional agriculture.

Although the French considered replicating ostrich ranching in West Africa, it was only in South Africa that ostrich farming took off, particularly in the Western Cape Province in the Karoo region, a large scrub desert the size of Texas. Located south of the Swartberg mountains in an area called the Little Karoo is Oudtshoorn, which in 1850 was a small agricultural town of no great prominence. However, it was soon to become the epicentre of the worldwide trade in ostrich plumes. For 60 years, from the 1860s to the 1920s, Oudtshoorn supplied ostrich feathers to London, Paris and New York.

Ostrich farming is particularly well suited to the hot, arid climate of the Karoo, which was already the home of the indigenous Southern ostrich. The first primitive farms for producing ostrich feathers for export were established there around 1863. It was easy to set up such a farm: all that was required was a parcel of land, a source of drinkable water and a few breeding birds whose first clutch of eggs could be augmented with eggs from the wild. A flock could be built up rapidly and provide a regular harvest of feathers. The only limit to expansion was the availability of natural vegetation for sustenance, but another great attribute of the Karoo was that it had the right soil and climate conditions to grow the legume lucerne or alfalfa, a food loved by ostrich.[3] The entrepreneurial farmers were often young, knowing little about the hardships of farming, their only comforts afforded by keeping a cow or two and the odd horse. Losing ostrich and livestock to wild animals such as lions and jackals was always a problem, so gradually the successful farms were enclosed with fences and pens.[4]

The next great innovation was replacing plucking with feather clipping. This improved production greatly, as it was much kinder to the ostrich. The quill was cut a few centimetres above the skin, avoiding damage to the follicles and allowing for a fresh crop of feathers every nine months. Clipping was a skilled job, because if the quill was cut too close to the skin it would bleed and prevent the proper regrowth of feathers. Three months after clipping, the dead quills could be removed without causing any pain to the bird. This was nonetheless always a risky task; the ostrich had to be restrained as a kick could easily break a bone or two, and the sharp claws could produce a deep cut. There are many stories of ostrich farmers being hurt or even killed at this time. However, once their heads were hooded the birds would stand still.

The number of ostrich farms grew quickly along with the demand from the European and American millinery industry. As the value of the feathers rose, feeding the birds with imported grain became economically viable, allowing larger and larger flocks to be kept, thus increasing feather production. The ostrich with the best feathers were selected and fed up for breeding stock.

The next innovation came in 1864 when the incubator was developed. This allowed three clutches of eggs to be hatched a year instead of two, allowing another step up in production. Ostrich thrived on the locally grown lucerne and farmers with enough land and irrigation could quickly become self-sufficient. While feather prices remained high, ostrich farming was a very attractive option. Apart from the British colonists and the Boer farmers already in the area, a new wave of settlers were attracted to Oudtshoorn, in particular Lithuanian Jews. In the late nine-teenth century there was mass migration of Russian Jews to Europe and North America, but for young entrepreneurs from a small region, around the towns of Chelm and Shalvi, the Karoo was particularly attractive because of their experiences of trading in the textile, tanning, hide, leather and fur businesses, and their connection to the fashion trade. These émigrés at first took up the role of dealing in feathers, buying them from farmers and selling them on to exporters in Port Elizabeth. Soon the most successful feather buyers bought their own farmlands and became successful producers in their own right. The rapid growth in demand ensured that prices remained high, and the feather producers soon became wealthy, building themselves grand mansions in the European style using imported materials from Europe and North America. During these boom years, Oudtshoorn, known as the Jerusalem of the south, was populated by several 'feather-millionaires'.[5]

While most of the ostrich feathers from South Africa were shipped to London, feathers from the so-called 'Barbary ostrich' in North Africa were traded through the Mediterranean ports. Feathers were often purchased before they were produced and feather merchants speculated on them and extended credit to intermediaries. With a bull market, this form of financing maximized profits. The feather merchants were largely Jewish in origin. A complex trading environment soon developed, a world described in fascinating detail by Sarah Stein in her book *Plumes* (2008):

> The Mediterranean Jewish feather trading diaspora: it was contingent on familial fidelity, conditioned by risk, sustained by credit, geographically peripatetic, and last but not least, navigated in Judeo-Arabic.[6]

With the rise of the British Empire and London at its centre, the capital became the main centre for feather trading as the Mediterranean centres gradually declined. A large number of feather workers lived in London, again mainly Lithuanian Jews. Feathers were traded in London and shipped to Paris and New York, where feather workers, again mostly Jews, trimmed, dyed and cut the feathers to make them into plumes.[7] Men were responsible for washing, bleaching and dyeing the feathers, which involved boiling them in cotton bags in vats filled with various chemical salts, like copper and tin.[8] Women would take the dried feathers and dress them; this was the most skilled of jobs. The feathers could be straightened and joined together.

After 1900 the demand for ostrich feathers reached its zenith. The fashion for hats and feather boas was huge. It was not just ostrich that were used but exotically coloured wild birds from all over the world. The sheer number of tropical birds killed and mounted on hats became of great concern to the naturalists of the time, and eventually in 1921 the Importation of Plumage (Prohibition) Act was passed, banning the trade in exotic feathers – apart from those of the ostrich and the goose, as these imports were sustainable. This was one of the first laws protecting the exploitation of wild animals.[9]

At the peak of the trend, feathers were South Africa's third most important export after gold and diamonds. The exponential increase in demand over the latter half of the nineteenth century was huge, as export and import figures show. In 1807, before ostrich farms were economical, 509 kg of feathers were imported into France; by 1913 South Africa in one year exported 464,000 kg, valued at £3 million and collected from over 1 million farmed ostrich.[10]

This big business needed to be protected by the South African administration. To this end the export of fertilized eggs and live ostrich was first heavily taxed and then banned. Other countries, including Australia and the USA, wanted to import the eggs and birds so that they could establish their own ostrich farms, but of course this would have harmed the South African fortunes.

The huge demand for feathers in South Africa had been met by rapid breeding of the Southern ostrich stock. At first this was from wild birds, but later birds were selectively bred for their

Workers in 1908 steam-cleaning ostrich feathers (above) and making feather crests (below).

Workers sewing
and trimming
feathers (above)
and making
feather boas
(below).

plumage. This led to a gradual improvement in the quality and quantity of feathers produced. Likewise, the Northern ostrich population became semi-domesticated, but was still mixed with the wild population. Some feather dealers noticed that the very best plumes came from North Africa; these were thought to come from the 'Barbary ostrich', a mythical sub-species of ostrich. These high-quality double-floss feathers were dense, springy and glossy and consequently commanded a dozen times the value of ordinary plumes.

In South Africa a group funded by the government decided to track down this elusive bird and bring a flock to the Karoo in order to produce a super ostrich, a hybrid cross between the Southern and Northern sub-species.[11] The detective work soon began, and British consuls from all over North Africa were asked secretly to send parcels of any locally sourced ostrich feathers they could find. This tactic soon paid off: a parcel from Tripoli contained the superior feathers, which had not come from the mythical 'Barbary' ostrich but a simple flock of sub-Saharan ostrich. The area in which the Arab traders had purchased the feathers in question was largely under French control. Even though the French fashion industry was one of the biggest users of ostrich plumes, the French had never seriously pursued ostrich farming. A secret plan was formed to obtain these superior North African or red-necked ostrich feathers. In a year a clandestine Trans-Saharan Ostrich Expedition (TOE) was formed and left Cape Town bound for London. In London the members of the TOE fitted themselves out for the long expedition to West Africa. As part of the preparations, Russell Thornton, age 30, their leader, visited Paris to glean more information about the particular double-floss feathers in question.

In September 1911 they left Southampton for Port Harcourt on the Niger delta in West Africa, from which they could begin the month-long journey north to the arid lands of sub-Saharan Africa. For the first part of the journey a steamer had been commissioned, taking them 500 miles up the river Niger to the city of Baro. From here the expedition travelled by rail to Zaria, the last railway station. Next the expedition proceeded on foot, assisted by over 100 local porters, to Kano on the edge of the Sahara desert. Kano was known as 'the greatest emporium in Africa'; trade routes from all points of the compass met there and it was the centre of the region's ostrich-feather trade. After befriending the local emir, the expedition set up camp and began inspecting as many of the feather bundles passing through as they could while trying not to raise too much suspicion. Eventually they found what they were looking for. Some Tuaregs had bought the sought-after feathers in an area west of Timbuktu in French West Africa. The expedition immediately journeyed to Zinder, the colonial capital, seeking permission to purchase and export a flock of ostrich. After a frustrating six weeks of waiting for a reply, the expedition received a resounding no. The French were not about to help the British. Not knowing what to do next, Thornton contacted Pretoria, requesting further instructions. After another six-week wait Pretoria replied, this time with a mixed response. While on the positive side £7,000 had been supplied to purchase the superior ostrich, the reply also stated that any purchases made would be the sole responsibility of Thornton and his team: in other words, Pretoria would deny all knowledge of financing the deal if it was ever discovered by the French authorities. The expedition immediately departed westward for Timbuktu, attracting the attention of the local tribes and French Legionnaires on the way. It was now December and the Harmatten, a dry and dusty trade wind, had arrived. The dust carried on this southerly wind blocks out the sun, causing temperatures to fall and making progress a real hardship.

To add to the intrigue, the expedition had been shadowed by a rival expedition bankrolled by a Californian consortium, whose aim was to purchase the same ostrich. The South Africans knew they were being followed, so as they headed towards Timbuktu they split into three groups and bought any ostrich they came across. This ruse worked, and the following expedition soon blew its budget on purchasing the same birds before triumphantly returning to the coast to ship their booty back to the USA. With their rivals gone, the TOE continued their search, eventually finding what they were looking for and purchasing 156 ostrich from a local emir.

This is where things became difficult. The big problem was now how to backtrack through the desert and get the birds home to Cape Hope. They couldn't just leave by the nearest French-controlled ports but had to retrace their journey back to Zaria, where they could pick up the railway. This was no easy task, since unlike cattle or sheep ostrich cannot be driven, so an ingenious solution was developed. Twenty mobile pens were crafted from palm leaves, each capable of corralling eight birds. The birds could be moved by four men, each carrying a corner of the pen. At nights the birds were released from their pens into 2-metre-deep pits dug into the sand. This system worked well and in May, following eight months of intrigue and travelling many hundreds of miles, they reached Lagos, where a ship was waiting to take the prize to South Africa.

The cargo ship ss *Ethiope* was not the best mode of transport, as it had no facilities for passengers, let alone adaptations for carrying livestock. The sea-passage was rough and the corralled ostrich did not stay on their feet easily. Ensuring that they remained upright required a 24-hour watch. To make matters worse, the supply of feed corn was reaching its end, and had to be supplemented with onions. Chopping onions and feeding and cleaning the holds became a full-time job. By 25 May Cape Town was in sight; 134 ostrich had made it to South Africa. Ahead was the last leg of the journey, a 400-mile train journey to the Karoo. Arriving at their final destination, disaster struck: the ostrich, sensing freedom, broke free at the very last minute and all escaped into the wilderness. Fortunately for the expedition, all but three of the birds were recaptured by nightfall.

Against all the odds, the TOE had been a great success. Eventually these birds were crossed with the best Southern ostrich to produce the black ostrich, *Struthio camelus var domesticus*, a superior bird. This produced a domesticated cross-breed whose descendants fill ostrich farms across the world.

In the nineteenth century New York City was still leading the U.S.'s fashion industry. Although no rival for London or Paris in terms of size, it still contained dozens of factories for dyeing and processing ostrich feathers. As in Europe, they were exclusively owned by Jewish families who employed mainly female Jewish immigrant workers. Working conditions were poor, especially in the sewing rooms. Apart from the long hours, the feather dust and ostrich dander constantly irritated the lungs, ears and throats of workers, leading to chronic lung disease and infections. Initially the feathers were imported from London but as their value grew the entrepreneurial Americans saw an opportunity to make money. The nascent agricultural industry was always looking for new products to grow or rear. The merits of ostrich farming were soon brought to the attention of the government, particularly as ostrich could be reared on arid land, one asset the Americans had plenty of.

Thus in February 1913 the Honourable Carl Hayden of Arizona addressed the House of Representatives in a bid to raise funding and encourage support for ostrich farming in the United States.

The ostrich remains preeminent as the bird against which there is no suspicion of ill-usage in yielding up its plumage. Whoever wears an ostrich plume is adorned with an emblem of justice. Wearing feathers from wild sources is cruel. The ostrich feather fulfils every legitimate need in the way of adornment – adornment obtained without the shedding the blood of innocents – and, if no other reason than this, the industry deserves encouragement by the American government.[12]

From a more commercial viewpoint it was calculated that by using feathers only from American sources $2 million more would stay in the country rather than be paid to foreign businesses.

The first American ostrich farm, the Cawston farm in South Pasadena, Los Angeles, was founded in 1886 and became the best-known of its day. Within a few years of its foundation, it was famed as a major tourist attraction, with visitors coming from all over the U.S. and the world. The farm's main purpose was producing feathers to sell individually or as boas, capes, fans and hats. Visitors could buy these at the on-site shop or by post, with the best 'comtesse plumes' costing $3.75 each. The farm boasted: 'Our feathers have more life, better curl, longer flues, stronger texture and greater weight than those produced elsewhere', further stating that 'no other climate of the world is so well adapted to the production of sturdy and luxuriant plumage'. The birds themselves also attacted visitors, who could ride in ostrich-drawn carriages around the botanical gardens on the grounds of the farm.[13]

The original ostrich stock for the farm had been quickly whisked out of South Africa the day before a law stipulating an expensive export duty, designed to prevent the export of ostrich and their eggs, was imposed. Although Edwin Cawston, the farm's founder, left South Africa with 50 birds, only eighteen made it to Pasadena. From these birds the American ostrich industry was founded. Farmers from across the U.S. were keen to establish ostrich farms, with Arizona and Florida having the most favourable climates. With all this interest and effort, ostrich numbers grew quickly: by 1896 there were around 700 ostrich living in the U.S., which rose to over 8,000 by 1913. In some places, particularly the more arid regions in Arizona, ostrich farming became more profitable than cattle ranching.

The booming feather industry continued into the twentieth century and allowed the spread of ostrich farming to the far

Oliver W., the famous trotting ostrich, Florida Ostrich Farm, Jacksonville, c. 1900–10.

corners of the world, particularly Australia and South America. But history tells us that periods of prolonged economic expansion cannot proceed for ever, and boom often leads to bust. The ostrich feather bubble finally burst after a radical change in fashion brought about by the First War World. The economic austerity associated with the war resulted in hats becoming smaller. Women's clothes became more functional as women started to work in industry and agriculture. More practical designs had no room for the ostentatious adornment offered by feathers. By 1913 the price of ostrich feathers had dropped by more than half and within a year around 80 per cent of all those with business interests in the feather industry were bankrupt. By the end of the First World War ostrich farmers could no longer make money. With little demand and few opportunities to transport feathers to Europe, the feather millionaires in their feather mansions in Oudtshoorn faced bankruptcy, some losing everything they owned, others still taking their own lives.[14]

After the collapse, feathers still adorned extravagant costumes, but only those found on stage and later in Hollywood films. While there was a brief revival in the 1920s following the discovery of Tutankhamen's treasures, the feather industry would never be as big again. The South Africans invented the ostrich feather duster in 1903 and some entrepreneurial Americans and Europeans manufactured feather dusters for their own domestic markets, finding the rougher black but fluffy bodyfeathers ideal for removing surface dust and cobwebs. The majority of these businesses were short-lived as the introduction of cheap synthetic materials made them too expensive. Eventually manufacturing ceased, although one company founded in 1913, the Beckner Feather Duster Company, survived. Today it leads a revival – albeit a small one – in the popularity of the ostrich feather duster.

Advertisement by the American Ostrich Company encouraging people to invest in an ostrich farm.

Strangely, no one at the turn of the twentieth century thought the ostrich was useful in any other way, even as a source of food. It was not until after the next world war that this view changed and a renaissance in ostrich farming began.

5   Ostrich *à la Carte*

Throughout the ostrich's long association with mankind, it has served as a valuable source of nourishment. The bird's ability to survive in semi-arid regions has provided local hunter-gatherers with a great source of protein in its well-muscled legs and its oversized eggs. The San people of the Kalahari, Namibia and the Western Cape, South Africa, used the eggs for food and the decorated shells as storage vessels. The empty shells, if they were smoked, became waterproof and, once stoppered, could be buried in the sand full of water in the wet season and recovered months later when water was in short supply. The San knew best how to exploit this resource and when they came across a nest they would never take all the eggs; they would always leave a few to ensure that the hens continued to lay.

The nomadic San also hunted and ate ostrich. They could not outrun the bird; nor were they able to approach closely enough through stealth alone to get within the range of their arrows. Instead they resorted to mimicry, impersonating their intended prey by covering their backs in old ostrich skins complete with feathers, neck and head.[1] With the hunter's legs exposed and his back covered, the skin's head was animated by inserting a spear or stick into the neck. Once attired, puppet-like, the costumed hunter would slowly walk towards the ostrich, trying to gain the bird's trust. The hunters were expert at making ostrich sounds

Ernst Philipp Thomann von Hagelstein, a group of hunters attacking ostrich with spears and dogs, *c*. 1700–26, mezzotint.

and imitating their behaviour. This allowed the hunter to slowly draw closer and closer to the birds. From under his costume he would then draw his bow and rapidly shoot as many ostrich as he could before the flock scattered and ran out of range. If the hunter killed even a single bird, the carcass would provide a good meal for everyone in the group, which ranged in size from ten to twenty members. Of course, this method of hunting was not risk-free: if the cock felt threatened by the approaching mimic he might attack the hunter, giving him a nasty kick. Hunters also used the ostrich costume to get close to other prey, since the ostrich is not considered a threat by its fellow creatures.

In their natural environment ostrich can easily outpace a horse and mounted rider. They are reported to have more stamina than a horse, which should make ostrich hunting very difficult, but the birds exhibit a peculiar response to being chased. Instead of running in random directions when chased, or even a straight line, an ostrich or flock of ostrich will run in an arc: in other words, if they are chased for long enough, they will run in a circle. Therefore all one hunter has to do is chase the birds while the other hunters wait for the birds to pass by. In the eighteenth century one European observer stated, 'it is a very pleasant Entertainment to hunt them for their awkward motions and unwieldy flight affords agreeable pastime to the hunters'.[2] Many prints from this period illustrate ostrich hunts. Typically they show the ostrich being either chased or attacked by a pack of dogs, with hunters mounted on horseback. Later, when hunters became armed with

An early 19th-century view of the ostrich in a stylized but unnatural habitat.

111

rifles, the ostrich became rather easy prey. Fortunately for the ostrich, this meant that the great Victorian hunters were not interested in it and left it alone. Those game animals that did run in straight lines when chased were slaughtered in their thousands.

The first texts to record whether creatures like the ostrich were edible were those written in Hebrew and listed in the Torah and later in the Bible. The Jewish culinary code defined whether an animal was clean to eat (kosher) or not. Mammals, such as the cow, had to be cloven-hoofed and omnivorous in order to be considered kosher, while in the category of birds, flesh-eating birds of prey and scavengers and songbirds were forbidden. This definition leaves the ostrich as kosher, since it falls into neither of these categories. However, in many versions of the Bible ostrich flesh is defined as non-kosher. In Leviticus 11:16 the ostrich is listed as an unclean bird, along with the gull, owl and hawk. The inclusion of the ostrich is now considered a mistake: a number of theories exist as to why it was reported as unclean. One theory was that the text could be describing a now-extinct species of Arabian ostrich that was more carnivorous than the remaining species. Alternatively the mistake could be due to a mistranslation of earlier texts, since the early name of the ostrich, *Struthio*, was shared with the sparrow, a songbird.

The Romans were not confined by these culinary laws and left plenty of evidence that they enjoyed eating ostrich. Preserved murals in the ruins of ancient Pompeii show people eating ostrich while Roman cookbooks list boiled ostrich as a food fit for a banquet. The Roman emperor Elegabalus (AD 203–222), famous for his extravagant banquets and debauchery, often served ostrich meat. He once famously ordered 600 ostrich heads for one banquet so he could serve ostrich brains to his guests.[3] Only wealthy Romans feasted on ostrich – it was a luxury, fit only for banquets, not an everyday food. The ostrich were imported, most probably alive, from North Africa along with other exotic birds like flamingos (which were also eaten boiled).

It is hard to establish when captive ostrich breeding and domestication began. Corralling wild birds was easy to do, as was collecting fertile eggs from nests; certainly ostrich breeding was practised in early nineteenth-century Libya. These breeding programmes were more likely intended to serve the ostrich-plume industry than culinary purposes, as slaughtering the birds for food is not worthwhile unless large breeding programmes are in place. Before the feather crash, ostrich meat was only a feature of the everyday diets of the indigenous peoples of Africa and Arabia. It was repeatedly reported that it wasn't worth eating. One ostrich-feather farmer reported that it was 'unpalatable', while another Edwardian writer stated, 'their flesh is hard and coarse, and one of their thighs resembles a leg of mutton, without being equally good'.[4]

It was not until the 1970s, when ostrich meat was declared fit for human consumption by the French government, that there was an explosion of interest in farming ostrich. People rushed to invest in ostrich farms and to capitalize on the price of fertile ostrich eggs. Speculators thought that they would make huge returns on their investment as the price of fertile eggs skyrocketed.[5] Investing in a pair of breeding ostrich or fertile eggs was the subject of several financial scams; potential investors were asked to invest up to $60,000 for a pair, and were promised profits of 20–300 per cent, since the birds were said to be such prolific breeders. Similar returns were promised on eggs that cost up to $5,000 each. Often the birds died or the eggs did not hatch and the money was lost. In the worst cases, the ostrich farms or ranches existed only on paper.

During these early days, the main issue for the potential ostrich farmer was creating a farm of sufficient capacity for enough

A Roman mosaic depicting the importation of ostrich.

breeding stock to produce subsequent generations for slaughter. These early pioneers underestimated how long it would take for production to become economically viable; another ostrich bubble was about to burst. Then, as if by a miracle, ostrich leather came to the rescue and within a short period became a 'luxury commodity', saving the day.

By 1992 South Africa was the biggest ostrich producer with 160,000 birds as farm stock; second was the u.s. with 15,400, then Israel with 8,000 and Zimbabwe with 4,000. This was still a fraction of the million or so birds farmed at the peak of the feather boom, 80 years earlier. Production increased with time and by 2001, 12–15,000 tons of ostrich meat was produced globally, with each bird producing around 30–40 kg of meat depending on its age and the production methods used. Farmed bird numbers had climbed to around 500,000 by 2003. By 2010 the Republic of South Africa was supplying 77 per cent of the global ostrich meat market, with 90 per cent of its exports shipped to countries within the EU. The economic value of producing 250,000 ostrich per year, reported by the South African ministry of agriculture, forestry and fisheries, is around $70 million, equal in value to its groundnut and rye crops. The income generated by the export of eggs and particularly leather doubles this amount. Fifteen tons of ostrich feathers are also sent to Brazil each year for making carnival costumes.

The economics of ostrich farming are attractive when compared to other livestock. A cow will only produce a single calf each year, which reaches the market after two years, yielding around 250 kg of meat. In just over a year a single female ostrich will produce around 40 chicks. Within a year these will yield around 1,800 kg of meat, 50 sq. metres of leather (compared to 3 from the cow) and 36 kg of feathers.[6] Thus a well-looked after ostrich, over the 30–40 years of her life, may indirectly produce up to 72 tons

Ostrich meat on sale in Beijing, China.

of meat, 2,000 sq. metres of leather and 1,450 kg of feathers, which all command high prices on the open market. Buying these products has never been easier and ostrich farmers can sell products directly to the public through the Internet as well as to larger commercial producers and supermarkets.

Ostrich meat is red and has a similar texture and taste to beef and veal, depending on the bird's age at slaughter. Weight for weight, ostrich meat resembles venison, but compared to beef and chicken it contains more protein and less fat and cholesterol. This means it has fewer calories as well, so ostrich meat can be a healthy alternative to these more common meats. Demand for ostrich is gradually rising around the world as the public gradually accept the idea of eating it. The turkey was originally seen as an exotic food, farmed and marketed for special occasions like Thanksgiving and Christmas, but the meat is now commonplace: the average American now consumes around 8 kg of it per year.[7] Ostrich meat can be marketed in a variety of ways, and when butchered can be supplied in ten different cuts. It can be made into fillet steaks, pâté and sausages, or even dried to make jerky or biltong. Ostrich can be used in many dishes and recipes, grilled, pan-seared, stewed, fried, roasted or braised. The number of ostrich farms continues to increase and, as production rises, supply to major food companies can be guaranteed. Many UK supermarkets plan to stock frozen ostrich cuts, while ostrich is already common on many restaurant menus. To many, the name 'ostrich' no longer invokes an image of the bird in its natural habitat, but a tasty steak. This is a feat also accomplished by other domestic fowl, such as the turkey, chicken, goose and duck.

Ostrich eggs are nutritious and taste sweeter than chicken's eggs. In South Africa native hunters would usually take the eggs from unattended nests but sometimes stole them from occupied nests by using a long, hooked stick. If eggs were stolen a few at

Making an ostrich-egg omelette.

a time, unnoticed by the hen, she would carry on laying more eggs day after day. In some cases she would produce over 50 eggs. At the fireside, the hunters would punch a hole in the top of the egg, stir the contents vigorously with a stick and roast it in the ashes; the resultant egg would have an omelette-like texture. In the days of sailing ships and long ocean voyages, on leaving the Cape of Good Hope, captains preferred to provision their ships with ostrich eggs rather than chicken's eggs as they were much stronger (easily supporting the weight of a grown man when stood end on), kept for longer and provided bigger meals for the crew.

Today ostrich egg production is another attractive area for farmers. Well-fed ostrich are good egg layers, and the average 1–2-kg egg, once cooked, produces a substantial family meal. Hard-boiling it takes 90 minutes, requiring forethought, planning and a big saucepan. Once boiled, the eggs are best opened using

117

a serrated knife. Equivalent to two dozen large chicken eggs, one ostrich egg will make an omelette for fifteen. This obviously has advantages for commercial establishments, but at around £20 per egg it remains a specialist food rather than a family favourite. British supermarkets have begun to stock ostrich eggs during the laying season, which stretches from spring to summer. Indeed, you can give someone an ostrich egg as an Easter gift. Ostrich eggs are high in unsaturated fatty acids and low in cholesterol, and are thus a good food for reducing cardiovascular disease.[8]

Another ostrich product is so-called ostrich oil, nowadays principally used to make a hard creamy soap. It has similar properties to avocado oil, and when added to shampoos, skin creams and soap provides a beauty product that commands a luxury price when appropriately packaged and advertised. The use of ostrich oil has a long history. The ancient Greeks, Romans and Egyptians used it as a skin cream and a remedy for arthritis. Pliny the Elder considered it finer than goose grease.[9] The oil – or, more correctly, the fat – is found between the skin and carcass, as ostrich muscle is largely fat-free. In times past the Arabs would collect the oil post mortem: after killing an ostrich they would slit its throat and then vigorously shake the carcass until around 10 kilograms of a bloodstained coagulated oil (called manteque) was collected.[10] Once separated and purified, the oil must be kept cool to prevent it going rancid. Today ostrich oil is still used medicinally and applied topically to treat a wide range of skin conditions and muscle fatigue. Ostrich oil contains a range of omega essential fatty acids which can penetrate the skin easily without clogging the pores.[11]

Ostrich oil production provided a valuable commodity after the feather crash in the early twentieth century, when many South African farmers were left with thousands of birds to feed and no market for their feathers. Slaughter was the only viable

A handbag made of ostrich leather by the French luxury brand Hermès.

option; as there was no market for ostrich meat or eggs, soap made from ostrich oil seemed to provide the answer. However, the demand for ostrich soap never became as vigorous as the one for feathers, so even this industry could not save many ostrich farmers from destitution.

Another by-product is ostrich skin or hide. Once tanned, this is thick, durable and very soft – some modern commentators say it is the softest and most durable leather on the market. It is now more valuable by weight than the feathers or flesh of the bird. Ostrich leather has been used throughout man's history. The Nasamones of ancient Libya made defensive shields from it, which they would carry into war, while Herodotus (484–425 BC) in his *Histories* informs us that the Macae used it to make shields.[12] This use continued into the nineteenth century, when Arab cuirasses or breastplates were still made of ostrich leather.[13] Although ostrich-skin tanneries have been operating in South Africa since the 1860s,[14] the international market was limited and did not expand with ostrich numbers. This changed in the 1970s when Texan cowboys decided that ostrich-skin boots were the ultimate in fashion.[15]

Ostrich leather is very distinctive because it is punctuated by the vacant feather quills. The price of the leather depends on the density of the quills, with 'full-quill' leather commanding the best price. The skin from the back makes the best leather.[16] Birds of around fourteen months old have skin of the right thickness, softness and pliability for use in footwear. Leather from younger birds is thinner and more suitable for clothes, whereas the leather from older birds is better made into belts. An adult ostrich can produce about 1.2 to 1.5 sq. metres of skin which, once graded for quality (as parasites, pecking and transporting the birds can damage their skins), has to undergo a month-long, three-stage tanning process. Perfected in South Africa, this is quite a smelly process that uses lots of water and produces a great deal of chemical waste.[17]

Since most of the world's ostrich-skin tanneries are in South Africa, the sale of ostrich leather has been intimately linked with the country's history. During apartheid the export of ostrich leather was closely regulated, making it very expensive. Following the establishment of the South African constitution in 1997, ostrich-leather production and exports increased dramatically as tanneries could now import skins from all over the world. Nowadays 215,000 skins are finished in South Africa each year. Most of this leather is then exported to the fashion houses of Europe, the U.S. and Japan, where it is often featured in the collections of Gucci, Prada, Hermès and Louis Vuitton. It is made into all manner of leather goods: as well as handbags, shoes and gloves, it is used to cover furniture and the interiors of luxury cars.

The ostrich is has always been susceptible to bird flu. In the past this was not a public health issue, as the commodities produced were worn rather than eaten. In the 1970s South African farmers began reporting that their free-range ostrich were suffering from respiratory problems during the winter. They had runny eyes and noses accompanied by a fall in egg production and a most peculiar fluorescent green urine. The cause was traced to an avian flu virus (H7N1).[18] Since then several strains have revisited the Little Karoo area. Observations showed that infection rates were at their worst when the birds were kept in crowded and unhygienic conditions. This led to improvements in husbandry and reduced rates of avian flu. Despite this, in 2004, 30,000 ostrich were culled in order to prevent an influenza virus pandemic; investigators found that the source of the infection came from a farmer who was keeping his birds in cramped conditions. The virus cannot be totally excluded, as it is introduced to farms by wild birds. The appearance of the virus coincides with the migration south of large numbers of sea birds from all over northern Europe and Russia. They arrive in early summer (October) and stay until autumn (March to April). While feeding in the wetlands of South Africa, they mix with local non-migratory water birds such as Egyptian geese. These, when grazing, can pass on the virus to the ostrich. This has led to suggestions by policy-makers that ostrich be kept apart from wild birds and given a separate water supply.[19]

In spring 2011 the export of ostrich meat to the European Union was suspended when a bird infected with the H5N2 influenza virus was discovered on a farm in the Oudtshoorn area. While the virus cannot be transmitted to humans and is destroyed by cooking, the worry was that it could easily mutate and affect poultry across the world. The export ban put a lot of pressure on farmers, as it was the end of the dry summer season and there was little feed left for the birds. Most would have been slaughtered for food. By 2012 over 40,000 birds had been culled in around 30 farms. During the ban, local consumption of the meat was allowed, as was the export of eggs, skins and feathers.

Ostrich farming is a labour-intensive endeavour, so with the closure of many farms unemployment levels rose quickly and

Farmed ostrich.

tourist levels dropped, creating an economic downturn similar to those seen in the town before. With so many of the region's birds culled it will take years to return numbers to their former levels. The problem of avian flu is not just limited to ostrich but is a problem for all bird farmers worldwide and is not likely to go away soon. Perhaps vaccination holds the answer: ostrich can be vaccinated against other avian viral diseases such as Newcastle disease, which has an 80 per cent mortality rate when left untreated.[20]

Ostrich farming or ranching occurs all over the world. The main centre is the Western Cape, where the bird is farmed principally for meat, but like elsewhere it is increasingly being farmed for its feathers, eggs, leather and oil. The success of any farming enterprise depends on the welfare of the animals, which in this

A herd of farmed ostrich.

case is reflected in the rate of egg production. A successful hen can lay between 30 and 100 eggs per season (the record is 167), and around 85 per cent of these will hatch. Taking into account chick mortality over the first three months, one chick is produced from every seven eggs laid.[21] The eggs are usually laid in damp, dirty conditions during the afternoon, so the eggs need to be cleaned before they are placed in an incubator. Here they are kept on their sides or upright at 36°C in a well-ventilated room with low humidity.

The chicks hatch at their own rate, some taking a few hours, other days. The chicks need to take their own time to allow the yolk-sac and its connection to be closed off in order to prevent fatal bleeding or infection. The newly hatched chicks are placed in brooders for a few days. Remarkably, they do not need food or water at this time, as they are still utilizing the yolk. The chicks are then moved to pens where they can scuttle around. Some farmers rear their chicks along with dwarf rabbits, as the new-born chicks see the rabbits as mother figures. The rabbits seem quite happy to live with the chicks and this temporary union improves their welfare: the rabbit droppings eaten by the chicks supply them with vitamins and introduce beneficial bacteria into their digestive systems.[22] The chicks are fed pelleted food but can also be given clover or lucerne.

The healthy chicks grow at a prodigious rate, and can double their weight during the first month, when they can weigh as much as 5 kg. By three months they will weigh 35 kg and at six months 65 kg. As long as they are fed a balanced diet containing at least 7 per cent of protein, the birds will continue to grow, and within a year can weigh as much as 100 kg.[23] Captive ostrich can suffer from deformed toes and legs owing to their fast growth, which can often be corrected by changing the diet or location of the birds. They suffer from external pests and internal parasites, plus a variety of diseases and bacterial and viral infections, which means they often require specialized veterinary care.

Sexing ostrich is possible at around one year old, and is useful because males are more important when producing feathers for market. A healthy ostrich should have alert eyes, glossy feathers, good feather cover, a rounded, well-muscled body and thighs, strong, straight legs and above all a good appetite.[24] Keeping both juvenile and adult birds requires a lot of space, and if kept in a temperate climate they must live in a barn during cold or bad weather. The pens must have good strong fencing that is high enough to prevent escape and injury, while the ground needs to be well drained and non-slippery. The birds need to express their normal behaviour for their age groups, and be kept away from stressors such as traffic noise and excessive numbers of farm visitors – although most of the ostrich I have seen seem just as curious about me as I am about them. A curious public is important, as many ostrich farmers supplement their income by advertising their premises to attract visitors. On some farms visitors can ride on the animals' backs and watch ostrich racing. Visits to the farm shop introduce the public to, and therefore popularize, new ostrich products.

In the 1990s, famine-stricken North Korea imported hundreds of ostrich in order to set up ostrich farms. They were to be run by cheap labour and ultimately provide cheap meat for the masses while at the same time creating a valuable export industry for the by-products. This vision never came to fruition and was soon abandoned, as North Korea is too cold for the ostrich. The surviving birds are seen more as pets by the current Communist leaders. Ostrich meat is only available at the finest and most expensive restaurants in the Pyongyang district, where all the country's leaders live. Vietnam has been more successful in farming the bird and many thriving ostrich farms can be found in the country. They supply the tourist trade with meat but also serve as visitor attractions, as in South Africa and the USA.

World demand for poultry is climbing and 2010 was a record year for production, with chicken, duck and turkey filling the world's supermarket shelves. The demand for ostrich meat, now widely recognized as a healthy alternative to beef, is following a similar trend. Ostrich farmers and breeders are gradually improving the genetics of their stock and with improved husbandry, the quality and quantity of meat is increasing. A sustainable supply will bring down prices, a necessary prerequisite for the major food suppliers and supermarket chains. The ostrich is still waiting for that 'turkey moment' when world sales take off and the general public begin to consider ostrich meat as ordinary as chicken.

6 Ostrich Symbolism and Imagery

Artistic representations of the ostrich, whether in petroglyphs, mosaics, drawings or carvings, have survived from ancient times. Decorated eggshell fragments that have survived for 60,000 years bear witness to man's earliest attempts at communication through art. The symbolic use of the ostrich as a cultural icon runs through the history of all the Middle Eastern, African and European civilizations, stretching back in time to their very beginnings. To the ancient Egyptians the ostrich symbolized trust and justice; to the Babylonians it was linked to evil; and to the early Christians it was an emblem of faith, certainty and rebirth.

This long history has ensured that the ostrich is found throughout man's cultural history, art, literature and language. In China recently discovered ostrich-eggshell beads and fragments which were drilled and stained 10,000 years ago provide evidence of early cultural development in East Asia.[1] In a Bronze Age site in Terqa, Mesopotamia, now in modern Syria, a tomb excavation has found ostrich-eggshell fragments which were placed as offerings to the two buried people in the tomb, suggesting that they were of high social status.[2] Over time dried ostrich eggshell becomes hard and shiny, and when gently polished it looks a lot like ivory, so it is easy to see how it became a valued object.

Ancient necklace
with beads made
of ostrich eggshell.

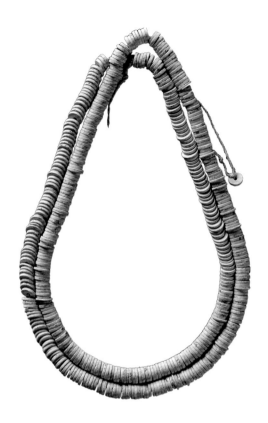

The finely crafted 40,000-year-old ostrich-eggshell bead necklaces found in the caves of Kenya's great Rift valley took a great deal of effort to make. They were probably not made solely for decorative reasons, as today in Botswana the Ju Hoan people use identical ostrich-eggshell bracelets as tokens of friendship and kinship. The exchange of bracelets supports a system known as *hxaro* which provides a sort of social insurance: someone in difficulty can call on other *haxro* partners for help or support when needed.

Earlier we saw how written descriptions of the ostrich became more realistic over time as their writers began to have more contact with living and captive birds. In medieval English literature the ostrich was well represented, though its name was more commonly spelled 'estridge', which remained in common usage until Victorian times. In Tudor England knowledge was still limited about the bird. Those characteristics described by the ancient Greek writers are illustrated in this amusing poem by John Skelton (1460–1529) from *The Boke of Phyllyp Sparowe*:

The estryge that wyll eate
An horshowe so great,
In the stede of meate,
Such feruent heat
His stomake doth freat;
He can not well fly,
Nor synge tunably.[3]

In the Elizabethan and Jacobean eras the estridge was alluded to in a similar fashion to how the peacock is today; because of its show of feathers, it had an air of vanity and showmanship about it. In 1600 Francis Bacon wrote to his friend, Robert Deveraux, 2nd Earl of Essex, who had recently been restored as Queen Elizabeth 1's favourite. He alludes to his downfall and restoration: 'For as I was ever sorry your lordship should fly with waxen wings, doubting Icarus's fortune; so for growing up of your own feathers, be they esteridge's or other kind, no man shall be more glad.'[4] The earl replied, 'I never flew with other wings than desire to merit and confidence in my Sovereign's favour.' This sentiment was not to last: the earl attempted rebellion and was subsequently executed for treason at the Tower of London in February 1601.

Edward VI with an ostrich feather in his hat.

In 'The Unfortunate Traveller, or the Life of Jack Wilton', written by the poet and pamphleteer Thomas Nash in 1594, Lord Henry Howard, Earl of Surrey, and his horse were both described as being 'all plumde like Estridges'; 'the trappings of his horse were pounced and bolstered out with rough plumed silver plush, in full proportion and shape of an estridge'.

Shakespeare used ostrich metaphors in his plays. In *Henry IV Part 1*, the ostrich appears in Sir Richard Vernon's speech describing how the prince and his knight companions, with plumes on their helmets, prepared for battle:

All furnish'd, all in arms;
All plumed like estridges, that with the wind
Baited like eagles having lately bathed;

Glittering in golden coats, like images;
As full of spirit as is the month of May. (IV, 1)

Here Vernon alludes to the idea that the flightless ostrich is swifter than the horse; its prodigious speed was then thought to be achieved by using its outstretched wings as sails. Shakespeare's heroes are spreading their wings magnificently, ready to catch the wind that will speed them into battle.[5] In *Henry IV Part 2*, Shakespeare also mentioned the bird's appetite for iron: 'I'll make thee eat iron like an estridge, and swallow my sword like a great pin, ere thou and I part' (IV, 10).

In Act III of *Antony and Cleopatra*, Antony's chief aide, Enobarbus, speaks: 'To be furious, is to be frighted out of fear, and in that mood the dove will peck the estridge; and I see still a diminution in our captain's brain.' The mildest of creatures, the submissive dove, will attack the greatest of foes, the ostrich, when in a paroxysm of rage.

The spelling 'estridge' continued to be used into the middle of the seventeenth century, as a poem from 1650 by Robert Heath shows: 'They have keen Estridge stomachs, and well digest both iron and lead, as a dog will a breast of mutton'. A transition from 'e' to 'o' then occurred around this time, estridge becoming ostridge; eventually by Victorian times the spelling finally became the one we know today.

The image of the ostrich inspired by the Bible appears in many fables and parables. In Aesop's 'Tale of the Eagle and the Kite', the female eagle is asked by a male kite why she is so sad, and replies that she has no mate. The kite suggests that he would make a good mate and boasts of his hunting prowess: 'Well, I have often caught and carried away an ostrich in my talons.' This obviously impresses the forlorn eagle and she accepts the kite as her mate. After the nuptials, she asks the kite for her ostrich as promised. The kite goes out hunting and returns with a mouse. Questioned why he has broken his promise, he replies: 'that I might attain your royal hand, there is nothing that I would not have promised'.

In another Aesop fable, 'The Ostrich and the Pelican', the ostrich comes upon a pelican with her chest all bloodied. The shocked ostrich enquires if the pelican has been savaged by some wild beast. The pelican quickly reassures the ostrich that she should not worry and explains that the wounds are self-inflicted; she is caring for her offspring by feeding them with her own blood. The ostrich berates her for sacrificing herself for her young. The ostrich advises that it is better to rely on providence, and proceeds to explain how she lays her eggs on the ground, leaving fate to decide which survive predation and accidents. She lets the warmth of the sun hatch the eggs, while nature provides food to the eggs. The mother ostrich does not need to nurture her young, and neither knows nor cares what happens to her offspring; thus she avoids any suffering. The pelican abhors this lack of parental care, telling the ostrich that the love engendered between a mother and her offspring is worth any sacrifice and a little suffering is of no consequence.[6] The bad ostrich is clearly an example of an irresponsible mother.

The ostrich appears in literature as an example of a creature that has a voracious appetite, or an iron constitution, but the most common reference of all is to its supposed habit of hiding its head in the sand to avoid danger from predators. This behaviour is parodied in a well-known quotation from the Irish poet Thomas Moore (1779–1852) in *The Sceptic: A Philosophical Satire* (1809), a poem exploring the issues of republicanism: 'Whole nations fooled by falsehood, fear, or pride / Their Ostrich-heads in self-illusion hide'. Another well-known quote is from Lord Macauley (1800–1859), who critiqued the poet John Dryden: 'His

The OSTRICH

BUSH of
RESIGNATION
bearing the
fruit of Repentance

The Ostrich and few will discredit Historians words,
Is the Higheft, the greateft, and rareft of Birds;—
Nor when prefs'd by the Hunters, he is ne'er known to fail
To hide his Head in a Bush; tho' he exposes his Tail;

With Hisses and Halloo's the Hunters deride
From his own guilty Confcience, he seeketh to hide;
Blend Truth with Conviction, if you've no diflike.
There is not a doubt, but t' is Moral will Strike—

Political cartoon of 1809 illustrating the Duke of York's resignation as Commander-in-Chief of the British Army. He is depicted as an ostrich attempting to hide in a bush as he is chased by John Bull.

imagination resembled the wings of an ostrich. It enabled him to run, though not to soar.'[7] Still in wide use today, the head in the sand metaphor is commonly applied in cases where politicians or business leaders ignore a situation in the hope that it will go away. A quick search of a few daily newspapers reveals other phrases derived from this belief: playing a perfect ostrich, adopting the ostrich approach and the ostrich game.

Jules Verne's hero Robur in *Robur the Conqueror* (1886) informs a riotous crowd: 'I have a constitution of iron . . . a muscular strength that few can equal, and a digestion that would be thought first class even in an ostrich!' In his *Dick Sand, A Captain at Fifteen* (1878), the somewhat naive hero of the story is shipwrecked in equatorial Africa, where he somehow gets confused between giraffes and ostrich when observing them from a distance. His wiser companions soon put him right, pointing out

The cover of the American satirical magazine *Puck*, captioned 'Protection', satirizing President Theodore Roosevelt's unpopular defence of an economic protectionist policy while ignoring calls for tariff reform (1904).

that one is a biped and the other a quadruped: the 'ostrich is only half a giraffe'.

Charles Dickens (1812–1870) makes great use of the many struthious (deriving from the Latin *struthio* and Greek *strouthos*, for ostrich) myths extant at the time: ostrich references are sprinkled throughout many of his novels. In *Little Dorrit* (1885), after the doctor examines the healthy Mr Merdle, he states: 'He has the constitution of a rhinoceros, the digestion of an ostrich, and the concentration of an oyster.' In *The Mystery of Edwin Drood* (unfinished at the time of the author's death) we see how 'Stoney' Durdles, the crypt-keeper and stonemason of Cloisterham Cathedral, 'drops his two keys back into his pocket one by one, and buttons them up; he takes his dinner-bundle from the chair-back on which he hung it when he came in; he distributes the weight he carries, by tying the third key up in it, as though he were an Ostrich and liked to dine off cold iron'. In *Martin Chuzzlewit* (1843), Mark Tapley, the younger Martin's manservant who accompanies

AIDS-awareness poster featuring an ostrich: 'Sticking your head in the sand won't help'.

him to America, describes the USA as 'like an ostrich, for putting its head in the mud and thinking nobody sees it'. (Dickens was disillusioned by the new American republic after touring the country and famously lampooned it in this book.) In *A Tale of Two Cities* (1859), 'The little narrow crooked town of Dover hid itself away from the beach, and ran its head into the chalk cliffs like a marine ostrich', while in *Great Expectations* (1860) 'It appeared to me that the eggs from which young Insurers were hatched, were incubated in dust and heat, like the eggs of ostrich, judging from the places to which those incipient giants repaired on a Monday morning.' In *Sketches by Boz* (1833), Dickens's first book, Miss Teresa goes to bed considering whether, 'in the event of her marrying a title, she could conscientiously encourage the visits of her parents' associates; and dreamed all night of distinguished noblemen, large routs, ostrich plumes, bridal flavours and Horatio Sparkins'. Dickens never seems to describe the bird itself in his extensive writing, using it only metaphorically, although he most likely would have seen living ostrich at London Zoo at the time.

In 1803 the poet Samuel Taylor Coleridge, in a confessional mood, wrote a letter to his friend Thomas Poole in a flamboyant style which contained the following allusions:

I lay too many Eggs in the hot Sands with Ostrich Care-lessness & Ostrich oblivion – And tho' many are luckily trod on & smashed; as many crawl forth into Life, some to furnish Feathers for the Caps of others, and more alas! To plume the Shafts in the Quivers of my Enemies and of them that lie in wait against my soul.[8]

These Coleridgean self-critical observations provide a window on the extent of the poet's vanity.

The ostrich's penchant for swallowing anything it can is used cleverly in an amusing short story about greed, 'A Deal in Ostriches', published in *The Stolen Bacillus and Other Incidents* in 1895 by H. G. Wells. The story is set on a steamer en route from India to London, which has on deck five captive ostrich. It begins with the premise that one ostrich has swallowed a valuable diamond from a Hindu passenger's turban. The ostrich-keeper, the owner of the turban and the other passengers discuss how they are going to recover it. Eventually, despite protests from the Hindu passenger, they decide to auction off the ostrich most likely to have swallowed the diamond. The successful bidder can then kill the ostrich and recover the jewel. The birds are auctioned off at ever-increasing prices to the various passengers, but no diamonds are found in their crops. Some time later, after the ship has docked in London, the ostrich-keeper and the owner of the turban are seen together, now the best of friends, the scam having earned them plenty of money. The story ends with the line, 'But whether the bird swallowed the diamond certainly is another matter, as you say.'

Twentieth-century usage of these literary struthious traits can be found in the works of the crime writer Agatha Christie. In *Five Little Pigs* (1943), the jealous murderer accuses the victim's wife: 'You're just like an ostrich that buries its head in the sand. You know perfectly well that Amyas and I care for each other.' In *A Caribbean Mystery* (1964), Miss Marple is reprimanded by her nephew Raymond on her old-fashioned views on sex: 'My dear Aunt Jane, why must you bury your head in the sand like a very delightful ostrich? All bound up in this idyllic rural life of yours. REAL LIFE – that's what matters.'

The Great Mosque of Djenné in Mali, built in 1907, is an impressive structure despite being constructed of wood and dried mud; it looks like a giant sandcastle with its high walls, towers and cone-shaped minarets. Close examination will show that placed on the apex of each minaret are two shiny ostrich eggs. To the Muslim worshippers the ostrich egg symbolizes fertility and purity. Ostrich nest in the spring as the rainy season begins – which marks the beginning of each new agricultural cycle – so it is easy to see the symbolic link. This symbolism is also true across the old habitats of the ostrich in the Arabian Peninsula and Indian subcontinent, and even today in India the ostrich egg finds it place in religious buildings.

In eastern Christian churches the ostrich egg was often either prominently displayed around the altar or more commonly suspended often by silver chains from the ceiling above the altar. The exact reason for this egg suspension is not known, but there are a raft of allegorical explanations for it: one suggests that because the ostrich is forgetful and leaves her eggs unattended, not returning until she sees the appearance of the star Virgilia, the eggs signify to man that he easily forgets God unless illuminated by a star, the Holy Spirit.[9] In another explanation, the belief that the ostrich hatched its eggs by gazing at them with some sort of heat-ray made the egg a symbol of God's perpetual attention. The eggs suspended in churches were treated as decorative ornaments but one anonymous scholar suggested that since the ostrich destroys bad eggs, the suspended egg is a warning to man: if he is bad, God will break him.[10]

At first these eggs were not decorated but gradually it became traditional to paint the eggs either with patterns or religious scenes. These were often given as gifts. Charles Dickens received

Mosque of
Djenné, Mali.

138

one as a gift from the Cape. In a letter to a friend he wrote that it was 'The most hideous ostrich's egg ever laid – wrought all over with frightful devices, the most tasteful of which represents Queen Victoria (with her crown on) standing on top of a church, receiving professions of affection from a British seaman.'[11]

Encasing the eggshell in elaborate gilded silverwork in the form of caps and bands became increasingly common; examples of this can be found in many museums across Europe. Gradually the egg became synonymous with Easter as a symbol of the Resurrection, birth and spring. Nowadays the chocolate Easter egg is a tradition familiar to many children, but few people appreciate the link between their extra-large ostrich-size chocolate egg and the ostrich and its origins in the deserts of Africa and Arabia. By the sixteenth and seventeenth centuries the decoration of the

Rubens Peale (1784–1865), *Basket of Peaches with Ostrich Egg and Cream Pitcher*, 1856–9, oil on canvas.

Piero della Francesca (*c.* 1415–1492), *The Brera Madonna* (also known as the *Pala di Brera*, the *Montefeltro Altarpiece* or *Brera Altarpiece*), 1472–4.

ostrich egg with gilded silver metalwork reached its zenith. Typically the egg was mounted on a highly ornate base and given a decorated top. As secular plate became less fashionable, goldsmiths and silversmiths created egg cups and covers with exotic themes associated with travel to tropical climes instead, incorporating ivory and exotic symbols such as pineapples into their designs. A fine example is owned by Queen Elizabeth ii and can be seen in the Royal Collection: a cup from 1623 made out of an ostrich egg, which incorporates silver into its design, given by the parishioners of St Mary Magdalene's, London, to Mr John Stopes, their parson's son. The decoration of eggs led to the creation by Fabergé of 50 fabulously bejewelled eggs between 1885 to 1917, made as Easter gifts for the Russian royal family. Today, decorated and carved eggs sold as works of art can still be found, especially in shops in South Africa, where they can sell for hundreds of rand.

OSTRICH PLUMES

Besides being used to decorate ladies' hats, ostrich feathers in the Victorian era were popular on the stage. They were used by female performers to enhance their stage presence. The music hall entertainer Florrie Forde (1876–1940) appeared with ostrich plumes fanned out like a peacock's tail behind her. By the early twentieth century the use of the ostrich feather fan had evolved into the fan dance, in which the fan is used to tease the audience by hiding bare flesh. This tradition has become part of the burlesque style and was enshrined at the world-famous Folies Bergère in Paris.

Meanwhile, across the Atlantic, in Hollywood the ostrich-feather fan and headdress became very popular components of costumes in big movie musicals such as *Top Hat* (1935), starring

A container made out of an ostrich egg and mounted in silver.

A Fabergé ostrich.

Dancer of the revue, Paris, 1937.

Prince William at a ceremony for the Order of the Garter.

Fred Astaire and Ginger Rogers. In Hollywood it was the job of the *plumassière* to create these magnificent feathery creations. Many were recruited from former feather factories following the post-First World War feather crash. Today one of the biggest users of ostrich plumes are the costumiers of carnival celebrations, such as those of the world-famous Rio de Janerio carnival and the Notting Hill Carnival in London.

The white ostrich feather is still also used on formal ceremonial occasions in Britain. One good example can be seen on St George's Day in April, when the Garter service at Windsor

Marlene Dietrich wearing an ostrich-feather boa in the film *Destry Rides Again* (1939).

145

Castle is held. This service is led by the monarch and her Knights of the Garter, who process to St George's Chapel dressed in ceremonial robes, topped off with elaborate Tudor hats adorned with magnificent white ostrich feathers.

Virtually all modern fashion designers use ostrich feathers to adorn their designs and any of today's popular fashion magazines will almost certainly show clothes decorated with ostrich feathers, often accompanied by ostrich-leather accessories. Although no longer the economic force it once was, the ostrich feather is still a popular fashion item and an icon of haute couture.

OSTRICH RACING

Very early in our history, it was discovered that the ostrich could be ridden, and was strong enough to support the weight of a bareback rider. Commentators from the eighteenth century mentioned that the indigenous populations from Niger could ride the birds. In 1759 one author, writing in the *London Magazine* on the 'surprising strength of the ostrich', reports how he tested the bird's strength by asking Nigerien locals of ever-increasing size to ride the ostrich. In the end the ostrich successfully carried two local tribesmen at once. He commented, 'I have frequently beheld this sight, which is capable of giving one an idea of the prodigious strength of an ostrich; and showing what use it might be of, had we but the method of breaking and managing it as we do a horse.'[12] While the writer considered the birds faster than horses, he thought they lacked stamina.

While horse riding does of course require technique and balance, riding a giant bipedal bird is a lot more difficult. The rider must sit upon the centre of the bird's back, equally balanced on either side of this pivotal point, else he or she will fall

Ostrich racing at a festival in California, 1998.

146

off backwards or the bird will fall over forwards. The neck is too flimsy to hold on to, and a small halter around the bird's head is the only thing the rider can grip. The ostrich does not obey instructions and, once mounted, will run off in any direction it chooses – often in a circle. Despite this unpredictability, ostrich racing still takes place. A large run is set up so that the birds have no choice but to run in one direction; when all are released at once, they race alongside each other. A spectacle, but perhaps not a sport, ostrich racing is common in the USA, and is a novelty that can be seen at festivals and at race tracks before the serious horse racing begins.

One of the longest running ostrich festivals is in Chandler, Arizona, a small town 170 miles north of Wilcox on the edge of the Chihuahuan Desert that was once at the centre of a large ostrich-farming area. The climate is very similar to the Karoo in South Africa, which made it an ideal site for rearing ostrich, first for their feathers and then more recently as food. In March, every year since 1989, hundreds of thousands of people visit the three-day ostrich and camel racing events, including ostrich chariot races. (Using ostrich to pull chariots or carriages dates back to Roman times, when it was popular among wealthy citizens. Emperor Firmus – who once boasted that he could eat a whole ostrich in one sitting – was a particular fan.)

Ostrich riding appears in the children's novel *Swiss Family Robinson* (1812) by the Swiss pastor Johann David Wyss. The book is about a family which gets shipwrecked in the East Indies. Although they would be more likely to come across cassowaries, the family members eventually encounter ostrich when exploring an arid region of their island. After killing one and later confiscating some eggs, they eventually capture one bird alive. A young member of the family tames it, and later uses it to ride and hunt with.

A recent children's story, *Ima and the Great Texas Ostrich Race* by Olivia McManis, illustrated by Bruce Dupree, is based on the great Texan philanthropist Ima Hogg (1882–1975), who kept two pet ostrich called Jack and Jill. In this inspirational story she races her ostrich against her two brothers on horseback.

The Walt Disney adventure film *Prince of Persia: The Sands of Time* (2010), set in ancient Persia, depicts an ostrich race, and the comedy film *Zookeeper* (2011) features Elmo, a talking ostrich, who offers the zookeeper a ride on its back, but finds him too heavy.

Searching through historical collections of children's literature will reveal many ostrich. *Denslow's Zoo* (1903) depicts the ostrich as a comical bird that takes children to the zoo by carrying them on its back. Many alphabet books and posters of the time used the ostrich to depict the letter 'O'. One rhyme from 1840 goes:

> O the ostrich, noble bird
> In Arabia's desert heard;
> Silly bird, in fear and dread,
> In the sand it hides its head.[13]

In Victorian and Edwardian books for young adults, the notion of hunting and making a fortune was presented as attractive, and setting up an ostrich farm in South Africa seemed to be the dream of many a boy. This is portrayed in the book *In the Land of the Lion and Ostrich: A Tale of Struggle and Adventure* (1897) by Dr Gordon Stables. In the nineteenth century the ostrich fulfilled many of the roles that wild animals do in children's fiction and non-fiction: it was regarded as exotic, strange and dangerous, and it could be hunted and killed like any game

A CONGRESS OF THE GIANT BIRDS OF THE WORLD, EMBRACING SPLENDID AFRICAN OSTRICHES,
ONLY LIVING SPECIMEN ON EXHIBITION OF THE AUSTRALIAN EMU: NEXT IN SIZE TO THE OSTRICH.
ASIATIC CASSOWARY OR HAIR BIRD, AND OTHER REMARKABLE BIRDS OF STRANGE AND BEAUTIFUL PLUMAGE.
NO OTHER MENAGERIE CONTAINS SUCH VALUABLE BIRDS. WE EXHIBIT THEM. NO OTHER SHOW DOES.

Ostrich were often exhibited in circus menageries, as demonstrated by this promotional poster of 1898: 'A congress of the great birds of the world'.

animal, but once domesticated it could be a pet or a farm animal and a valuable product.

The heightened growth of children's book publishing coincided with the colonization of Africa by Europeans, which involved lands that were the main dominion of the ostrich. Ostrich 'became metaphors and symbols not only for those who glorified what was being done to the country but also those who questioned it'.[14] The *Young Yägers* (1857) by Captain Mayne Reid largely tells the story of the adventures of a group of young hunters who have several encounters with ostrich during their expeditions; consequently the book contains a lot of factual information about the ostrich. Potential danger from the ostrich is a theme used in many such novels and the lethal ostrich kick was often used as a plot device. 'Shoot, man, shoot! They say a black ostrich that's guarding his nest will kick your horse to ribbons, and then have a good go at you before he stops.'[15] This theme was also used in *A Girl of Distinction* (1912) by Bessie Marchant and in *Corah's School Chums* (1912) by May Baldwin.

FINE ART

Young Couple Threatened by Death, an engraving of 1498 by Albrecht Dürer, shows a young beau wearing a large ostrich plume in his hat, a precursor to the feathered caps that became popular in the sixteenth century and were worn by the Tudors. In this highly allegorical work the youth is directing his young love along a path ahead, a metaphor for the couple's future life together; the feather is used to symbolize his bachelorhood. In the background, behind a tree, Death hides unnoticed, holding an hourglass, providing a moralizing metaphor for the ephemeral nature of love and sensuality.

Ostrich can be found in fresco paintings in Madrid, Rome and Padua. In the fifteenth-century Padua fresco the ostrich is included in a panel representing January, an association also used in later works of art. In Rome a fresco created by Romano Giulio (1492–1546), on the wall of the Camera con Fregio di Amorini (Chamber of the Cupid Frieze) in the Villa Madama, depicts a rather drab ostrich with a lowered head against a white background – a rather unusual subject. While in Spain, on the ceilings of the Throne Room in the Royal Palace, the image of a majestic male ostrich is shown overlooking a Moorish or North African panorama in one of a series of scenes depicting the Glory of Spain, painted in 1764 by Giovanni Battista (1696–1770).

The ostrich appeared in many European works of art of the
sixteenth and seventeenth centuries. The Flemish Baroque painter
Roelandt Savery (1576–1639), who included birds in many of
his paintings, often depicted the ostrich. One work, *Landscape
with Birds*, shows a pair of ostrich standing on a promontory
overlooking a menagerie of birds, including a dodo, from all
over the known world. In his depictions of the Garden of Eden
and Noah's Ark, the ostrich appears in various guises. The bird
usually appears either on the left or the right of the picture, its

Roelandt Savery,
*Landscape with
Birds*, 1628,
oil on panel.

long, vertical shape making it the ideal creature to fit these spaces, while its presence there added a modicum of exotica to the works. Other contemporary artists also included the ostrich in their works, notably Jan Brueghel the Elder (1568–1625). His renditions of ostrich were particularly lifelike and reflect his knowledge of Renaissance zoology.

Another popular subject which includes the ostrich is Orpheus charming the animals. Orpheus was renowned for his ability to communicate with all manner of creatures. In these artworks the ostrich often appears, standing next to a horse or a cow. The association of the ostrich with Orpheus may date from classical times: a Roman mosaic from Palermo shows Orpheus surrounded by a variety of animals, including an ostrich. Allegorical paintings

from Roman times also include the ostrich. In *An Allegory of Air* by Ferdinand Van Kessel (1648–1696) the flightless ostrich is set against dozens of smaller flying birds, which are shown gliding graciously through the sky along with winged cherubs. Surprisingly, in *Tropical Birds in a Landscape* the same artist's representation of a pair of ostrich is not true to life. When artists choose to make the ostrich the central focus of their work, as in *Exotic Birds and an Owl on the Banks of a River* by J. F. Hefele (*d.* 1710) and *An Ostrich* by Francis Barlow (1626–1702), the inaccuracy of their detailing becomes more apparent.

154

MODERN MEDIA

A cartoon ostrich served an important role in the Second World War, providing a propaganda foil against Nazi Germany. In July 1938 the British children's comic *The Beano* launched its first edition. The character on its front cover was Big Eggo the Ostrich, a comical but somewhat ugly and scatterbrained bird who lived on an island with his animal friends. In the first stories Big Eggo was mainly concerned with protecting his eggs (despite there being no female ostrich), and in the very first strip he ends up mistakenly incubating a crocodile's egg. Upon hatching, it rather ungratefully bites Eggo. Later, as Reg Carter, his creator and artist, became more ambitious, Big Eggo evolved and moved

An ostrich in J. F. Hefele, *Exotic Birds and an Owl on the Banks of a River*, early 18th century.

155

THE BEANO COMIC

No. 279. JAN. 12th, 1946

2D

into an urban environment. He was transformed into a 'brainy bird' with a pair of Mickey Mouse-like hands attached to his wings, and with a voice. Eggo was now able to outwit any adversary including Hitler's army, and in one strip he singlehandedly captures a German U-boat. After 326 issues over eleven years, Eggo was superseded on the front cover by Biffo the Bear, and he retired on Carter's death in 1949. Looking at the first cartoons, it is remarkable that Big Eggo was thought able to provide enough variety of material for a weekly comic, but the trials of war soon gave the ostrich plenty to do.

Another famous ostrich character is Ossie the ostrich, a pink puppet well known to Australian children who appeared on television for two decades in the 1970s and '80s. Ostrich characters are not so common today, but they are plentiful in the film *Madagascar Escape 2 Africa* (2008), and the ostrich Mr Ping can be found in *Kung Fu Panda 2* (2010). 'Olive the Ostrich' is a popular pre-school children's television programme in the UK.

The ostrich is universally recognized across the globe, and with its strange, gawky appearance, it makes an ideal comic figure in advertisements. One of the best-known adverts to star the ostrich is for Guinness, created as part of a series by John Gilroy in the 1930s; it shows a zookeeper with an ostrich which has swallowed a whole glass (presumably full of Guinness) that is lodged halfway down its neck. In an American public health campaign of the 1980s the ostrich, shown with its head buried in the sand, was used to raise awareness of AIDS. The message was that ignoring AIDS would not cause the problem to disappear. Recently, in a Cadbury's chocolate advert, an ostrich was shown jumping out of the back of a transporter plane and elegantly gliding through the air with her wings spread before opening her parachute to land. The advert's message was that

A 'Big Eggo' cartoon in *The Beano* (1946).

the joyous experience of eating chocolate equates to the joy that the ostrich would feel if it could fly through the air.

The ostrich appears in many adverts for circuses and zoos but rarely in adverts that promote safaris. Although just as impressive as any of the 'big five' game animals, it is evidently not considered symbolic of the great African plains.

OSTRICH IN NAME ONLY

While ostrich appears on the menus of many restaurants, there are several inns in the UK named after the ostrich itself. Most are found along the Welsh–English border and in the Fens. In most cases the names reflect a link to the Prince of Wales's triple-plume crest, so the Welsh connection is obvious. The connection to the Lincolnshire, Norfolk and Cambridgeshire area is less clear, but lands there were owned by the Prince of Wales in medieval times.

The Ostrich Inn in Colnbrook, Berkshire, dates back to 1106 and claims to be one of England's oldest. It became infamous when in 1624 the landlord was found guilty of murdering thirteen guests while they slept, purely for financial gain. Another famous Ostrich Inn can be found in Redcliffe, Bristol. It is little changed since it was built in 1745. It sits on the quayside, and originally served the sailors, sea captains, merchants and dock workers involved in the slave trade. The Feathers Inn, built in 1619 in Ludlow, situated in Shropshire in the Welsh Marches, is notable for its Jacobean timber facade decorated with a carved ostrich-feather motif.

The surname Ostrich is not common but can be found in the UK and USA: there are more people with the surnames Estridge and Ostridge, derived from the old spellings. The German word for ostrich, *Strauss*, is a more common surname, not only in Germany but across the world. One of the earliest records of the surname Ostrich is of a Tudor family based in London. Thomas Ostrich (*d.* 1483) was a well-known London haberdasher. Court records show him to be a litigious man; he was often in the Court of Chancery, disputing the ownership of various parcels of land, even taking proceedings against his own mother, Amy Ostrich. We know that his daughter Margery married Ralph Astry, the Mayor of London. Being a haberdasher, he traded with textile merchants in Ghent, and was one of the first traders to pay for goods using credit notes. His two sons, Henry and William Ostrich, continued in the business and mixed with the royal court, with Henry receiving an annuity of £40 from Edward VI in 1550.[16] Henry, along with a syndicate of other merchants, tried to set up trade links with Morocco, which would provide a valuable source of ostrich plumes for royal haberdashery. A portrait of Edward VI shows the king wearing a white ostrich plume in his hat (see p. 130). A contemporary entry from the Port of London show that in 1568, 125 lbs (57 kg) of ostrich feathers were worth £237.

Later when, Mary I ascended the throne, British trade routes were extended to the west coast of Africa, where ostrich feathers were traded, among other goods. Apart from these expeditions Henry Ostrich was involved with the Privy Council in planning the exploration of the polar regions by Sebastian Cabot, who later went on to explore North America. Further records show that William Ostrich was given £66 to apprentice Robert and Nicholas Thorne, the illegitimate sons of the Bristol merchant Nicholas Thorne (1496–1546) the founder of the Bristol Grammar School. His motto, 'Ex spinis uvas', translates as 'From thorns, grapes'; 'thorns' a reference, it is thought, to the founding family, the Thornes.[17]

The ostrich, although not a maritime bird, has given its name to many nautical vessels, both merchant and naval. In December

1759, during a violent storm off the south coast of Devon and Cornwall, the ship the *Estridge* was wrecked on the rocks; its captain, Robert Wyham, and the crew all drowned. During the American War of Independence, in 1778, HMS *Ostrich*, a fourteen-gun sloop under Captain Peter Rainer, captured an American privateer. The following year it took part in the Battle of Narragansett Bay, Rhode Island, where Lt General Lord Charles defeated the American forces commanded by Major General Gates. The ship was decommissioned in 1782. The second HMS *Ostrich* was a 375-ton gypsy class destroyer launched in 1900, which was in service for twenty years. There have been three USS *Ostrich*: the first was commandeered in 1917 during the First World War and was returned to its owner Nathan Strauss in 1918. Whether the owner's name influenced the U.S. Navy's name for the ship is not recorded. The second USS *Ostrich* saw service in the Second World War. Launched in 1941, it patrolled the eastern coastline of the U.S. and then the gulf coastline before being scrapped in 1946. The third USS *Ostrich* was a minesweeper, seeing service in Hawaii, Japan and along the east coast of the U.S. After being used as a survey ship, it was finally decommissioned in 1958.

In 1854 the three-masted barque *Ostrich* took 93 days to sail from Southampton to Adelaide, Australia. The ship carried 'government' passengers, consisting of emigrating tradesmen and their families. On the journey there were four births and four deaths. In 1876 the merchant vessel SS *Ostrich* collided with SS *Benbow* and sank, killing four passengers and one fireman.[18]

A LONG-NECKED BIRD

Although not endangered as a species, you will find a flock of ostrich in most large zoos. Unfortunately it is usually the domesticated hybrid that is on display and little attention is paid to rearing the remaining rarer African sub-species. Always popular and easily identifiable, the birds are easy to keep and will co-exist happily with other birds and animals like giraffe, zebra and antelopes. This reinforces the view that the ostrich is still considered by the public as a 'wild beast', not a farm animal.

The ostrich is unique in many ways: a giant among birds; a single species occupying its own special niche in the natural world; a biological miracle, evolved to withstand the harshest of environments. While the ostrich has shared its history with man since the Stone Age, its indestructible eggshells have left an indelible record of man's early attempts at art and written communication. Populating North Africa and the Middle East, the ostrich was well known to ancient naturalists, and its habits and mannerisms were transcribed into many ancient texts such as the Bible. This religious association became more engrained as the ostrich eggshell became part of religious iconography. In the Middle Ages the bird was relatively unknown in Europe and has consequently only left a minor impression, and would have remained on the periphery of our cultural history were it not for its feathers. Being flightless allowed the ostrich to follow a different evolutionary route to other birds, allowing its feathers to evolve into the ridiculous, flossy and elegant feathers we value today. Over time these feathers became increasingly sought after, and particularly valued, providing knights with decorations for their helmets, and others for their hats and caps, providing that extra special touch of class, desired by the rich and powerful. As this demand grew, and the ostrich feather was adopted as a fashion item for the masses, the numbers of ostrich shrank in direct proportion, and it would have faced extinction in the wild had it not been for its ultimate domestication as a farm animal. (A story that, in a strange way, proves Charles Darwin's maxim regarding the survival of the fittest: by becoming flightless and producing

feathers that do not provide camouflage, the ostrich would serve another purpose, feeding the vanity and stomachs of men.) Nowadays the domesticated ostrich provides a range of products, giving farmers across the world a living and consumers ever-increasing culinary and fashion choices. The ostrich is a worldwide phenomenon and now firmly enmeshed in our culture not only as a metaphor of indecision but also as a supplier of elegant leather, plumes and meat. It truly is a giant among birds.

Two ostrich at a waterhole in Etosha National Park, Namibia.

Timeline of the Ostrich

170 MILLION YEARS AGO

An early common ancestor begins to diverge as Gondwana splits

80 MILLION YEARS AGO

The modern ratites, a group of flightless birds, evolve

4TH CENTURY BC

Aristotle describes the ostrich

1ST CENTURY BC

First written records of the ostrich by the Chinese

3RD CENTURY AD

Roman emperor Elegabalus serves 600 ostrich brains at a banquet

1863

First farms dedicated to the production of ostrich feathers are established in South Africa

1913

The great ostrich-feather industry crash occurs

1938

Big Eggo the Ostrich features on the cover of the first issue of *The Beano* comic

| 20 MILLION YEARS AGO | 60,000 YEARS AGO | 1323 BC |

The first fossil record of the African ostrich

Decorated ostrich-eggshell fragments found at the Diepkloof Rock Shelter in South Africa date from this period

Tutankhamen's tomb contains ostrich imagery

| 1070 | 1346 | 1599 |

Ostrich depicted in the Bayeux Tapestry

After the Battle of Crécy, the Prince of Wales adopts the ostrich plume in his coat of arms

Ulisse Aldrovandi publishes his *Ornithologiae* with illustrations of ostrich

| 1966 | 1970 | 2011 |

Arabian ostrich becomes extinct

Ostrich meat declared fit for human consumption in Europe

Bird flu leads to the deaths of 40,000 ostrich in South Africa

References

1 FLIGHTLESS BIRDS, EXTINCT AND EXTANT

1 T. H. Huxley, 'On the Classification of Birds; and on the Taxonomic Value of the Modifications of Certain of the Cranial Bones Observable in that Class', *Proceedings of the Zoological Society of London*, CXLV (1867), pp. 415–72.

2 Graham E. Budd, 'Royal Fossils: The Royal Society and Progress in Palaeontology', *Notes and Records of the Royal Society*, LV (2001), pp. 51–67.

3 Charles Darwin, *The Origin of Species by Means of Natural Selection*, 6th edn (London, 1872).

4 R. Owen, *The Anatomy of Vertebrates*, vol. II: *Birds and Mammals* (London, 1871).

5 Alan Cooper et al., 'Complete Mitochondrial Genome Sequence of Two Extinct Moas Clarify Ratite Evolution', *Nature*, CDIX (2001), pp. 704–6; John Harshman et al., Phylogenomic Evidence for Multiple Losses of Flight in Ratite Birds', *Proceedings of the National Academy of Sciences of the USA*, CV (2008), pp. 13,462–7.

6 Matthew J. Phillips et al., 'Tinamous and Moa Flock Together: Mitochondrial Genome Sequence Analysis Reveals Independent Losses of Flight Among Ratites', *Systematic Biology*, LIX (2010), pp. 90–107.

7 Leona M. Leonard, Gareth J. Dyke and Cyril A. Walker. New Specimens of a Fossil Ostrich from the Miocene of Kenya', *Journal of African Earth Sciences*, XLV (2006), pp. 391–4.

8 Errol Fuller, *Extinct Birds* (Oxford, 2000), p. 398.

9 D. T. Potts, 'Ostrich Distribution and Exploitation in the Arabian Peninsula', *Antiquity*, LXXV (2001), pp. 182–90.

10 J. M. Miller et al., 'Phylogeographic Analysis of Nuclear and mtDNA Supports Subspecies Designations in the Ostrich (*Struthio camelus*)', *Conservation Genetics*, VII (2010), pp. 423–31.

11 Nicolas Manilus, 'The Ostrich in Egypt: Past and Present', *Journal of Biogeography*, XXVIII (2001), pp. 945–53.

12 Aerial total count, Wet Season, March 2010. Report by the Kenya Wildlife Service and Tanzania Wildlife Research Institute; J. O. Ogutu et al., 'Continuing Wildlife Population Declines and Range Contraction in the Mara Region of Kenya during 1977–2009', *Journal of Zoology*, CCLXXXV (2011), pp. 99–109.

2 FORM, FUNCTION AND HABITAT

1 Z. Brand and S.W.P. Cloete, 'Genetic Parameters for Feather Weights of Breeding Ostriches', *Proceedings of the Association for the Advancement of Animal Breeding Genetics*, XVIII (2010), pp. 488–91.

2 Alexander Macalister, 'On the Anatomy of the Ostrich (*Struthio camelus*)', *Proceedings of the Royal Irish Academy*, IX (1864), pp. 1–24.

3 Dzemski Gordon and Andreas Christian, 'Flexibility Along the Neck of the Ostrich (*Struthio camelus*) and Consequences for the Reconstruction of Dinosaurs with Extreme Neck Length', *Journal of Morphology*, CCLXVIII (2007), pp. 701–14.

4 Arthur Trevenning Harris, 'Nitwits in Feathers', *The Saturday Evening Post* (24 December 1949), p. 19.

5 Kemei Peng, Weimin Zhang and Yueping Feng, 'Anatomical Research on the Brain of African Ostrich', *Journal of Huazhong Agricultural*, IV (1998).

6 John A. Lesku et al., 'Ostriches Sleep Like Platypuses', *PLoS One* (2011), VI/8, e23203.

7 D. Boire, J. S. Dufour, H. Théoret and M. Ptito, 'Quantitative Analysis of the Retinal Ganglion Cell Layer in the Ostrich, *Struthio Camelus*', *Brain, Behavior and Evolution*, LVIII (2001), pp. 343–55.

8 Aghdas Poost Pasand, Mina Tadjalli and Haldi Mansouri, 'Microscopic Study on the Tongue of Male Ostrich', *European Journal of Biological Sciences*, II (2010) pp. 24–31.

9 Gary E. Duke, A. Allen Degen and James K. Reynhout, 'Movement of Urine in the Lower Colon and Cloaca of Ostriches', *The Cindor*, XCVII (1995), pp. 165–73.

10 Joseph B. Williams et al., 'Field Metabolism, Water Requirements and Foraging Behaviour of Wild Ostriches in the Namib', *Ecology*, LXXIV (1993), pp. 390–404.

11 Jonas Rubenson et al., 'Adaptations for Economical Bipedal Running: The Effect of Limb Structure on Three-dimensional Joint Mechanics', *Journal of The Royal Society Interface*, VIII (2001), pp. 740–55.

12 Rebecca Watson et al., 'Gait-specific Energetics Contributes to Economical Walking and Running in Emus and Ostriches', *Proceedings of the Royal Society B: Biological Sciences*, CCLXXVIII (2011), pp. 2,040–46.

13 Nina Ursula Schaller et al., 'Toe Function and Dynamic Pressure Distribution in Ostrich Locomotion', *The Journal of Experimental Biology*, XXXIV (2011), pp. 1,123–30.

14 Nicola Smith, Karin J. Jespers and Alan M. Wilson, 'Ontogenic scaling of locomotor kinetics of the ostrich (*Struthio camelus*)', *The Journal of Experimental Biology*, CCXIII (2010), pp. 1,347–55.

15 Knut Schmidt-Nielsen et al., 'Temperature Regulation and Respiration in the Ostrich', *The Condor*, LXXI (1969), pp. 341–52.

16 Eugene Crawford, 'Temperature Regulation and Evaporative Cooling in the Ostrich', *American Journal of Physiology*, CCXII (1967), pp. 347–53.

17 James Jones, 'Pulmonary Blood Flow Distribution in Panting Ostriches', *Journal of Applied Physiology*, LIII (1982), pp. 1,411–17; Schmidt-Nielsen et al., 'Temperature Regulation and Respiration in the Ostrich', pp. 341–52.

18 P. K. Phillips and A. F. Sanborn, 'An Infrared Thermographic Study of Surface Temperature in Three Ratites: Ostrich, Emu and

Double-wattled Cassowary', *Journal of Thermal Biology*, XIX (1994), pp. 423–30.

19 Schmidt-Nielsen et al., 'Temperature Regulation and Respiration in the Ostrich'.

20 R. G. Cooper et al., 'The Wild Ostrich (*Struthio camelus*): A Review', *Tropical Animal Health and Production*, XLI (2009), pp. 669–78.

21 Christopher Perrins, ed., *The Encyclopedia of Birds* (Oxford, 2009), pp. 34–7.

22 Flora J. Magige et al., 'Breeding Biology of Ostriches (*Struthio camelus*) in the Serengeti Ecosystem, Tanzania', *African Journal of Ecology*, XLVII (2009), pp. 400–08.

23 C. N. Kimwele and J. A. Graves, 'A Molecular Genetic Analysis of the Communal Nesting of the Ostrich (*Struthio camelus*)', *Molecular Ecology*, XII (2003), pp. 229–36.

24 C. R. Thouless, J. H. Fanshawe and B.C.R. Bertram, 'Egyptian Vulture (*Neophron percnopterus*) and Ostrich (*Struthio camelus*) Eggs: Origins of Stone-throwing Behaviour', *Ibis*, CXXXI (1989), pp. 9–15.

25 Flora J. Magige, Børge Moe and Eivin Røskaft, 'The White Colour of the Ostrich (*Struthio camelus*) Egg is a Trade-off between Predation and Overheating', *Journal of Ornithology*, CXLIX (2008), pp. 323–8.

26 Nicola C. Smith, Karin J. Jespers and Alan M. Wilson, 'Ontogenetic Scaling of Locomotor Kinematics of the Ostrich (*Struthio camelus*)', *The Journal of Experimental Biology*, CCXIII (2010), pp. 1,347–55.

3 CAMEL-BIRD

1 Pierre-Jean Texier et al., 'A Howiesons Poort Tradition of Engraving Ostrich Eggshell Containers Dated to 60,000 Years Ago at Diepkloof Rock Shelter, South Africa', *Proceedings of the National Academy of Sciences*, CVII (2010), pp. 6180–85.

2 Chester Cain, 'Implications of the Marked Artefacts of the Middle Stone Age of Africa', *Current Anthropology*, XLVII (2006), pp. 675–81.

3 Sven Ouzman, 'Twyfelfontein Site Report: Namibia Rock Art Africa', at www.bradshawfoundation.com, accessed 22 October 2012.

4 P. V. Tobias, T. A. Dowson and J. D. Lewis-Williams, '"Blue Ostriches" Captured', Nature, CCCLVIII (1992), p. 185.

5 Aristotle, *Parts of Animals*, trans. A. L. Peck (Cambridge, MA, 1959).

6 Berthold Laufer, *Ostrich Egg-shell Cups of Mesopotamia and the Ostrich in Ancient And Modern Times* (Chicago, 1926); A. H. Godbey, 'Sisinnu = "Horsebird" = Ostrich', *The American Journal of Semitic Languages and Literatures*, CC (1904), pp. 257–9.

7 Laufer, *Ostrich Egg-shell Cups*.

8 Ibid.

9 Dale J. Osborn, 'A Rebuttal of Criticisms of Identifications of Animals Portrayed in the Tomb of Tutenkhaum', *American Journal of Archaeology*, LXXXIX (1985), pp. 157–61.

10 Marina Belozerskaya, *The Medici Giraffe, and Other Tales of Exotic Animals and Power* (New York, 2006).

11 Panel 54/53. W. Brunsdon Yapp, 'Animals in Medieval Art: The Bayeux Tapestry as an Example', *Journal of Medieval History*, XIII (1987), pp. 15–73.

12 Ibid.

13 W. Brunsdon Yapp, 'The Birds of English Medieval Manuscripts', *Journal of Medieval History*, V (1979), pp. 315–48.

14 Conrad Gesner, *Historia animalium*, 1st edn, vol. III (1555), p. 708.

15 Roy Strong, *Gloriana: The Portraits of Queen Elizabeth I* (London, 2003).

16 Belozerskaya, *The Medici Giraffe*.

17 British Museum, London, UK. Print by J. Carwitham (1741). Reg. No. 1914,0520.484.

18 Stuart Andrea, *The Rose of Martinique: A Life of Napoleon's Josephine* (London, 2003).

19 P. Dixon Hardy, 'The Dublin Zoological Society', *The Dublin Penny Journal* (5 April 1834), vol. II, pp. 313–18.

20 'List of the animals in the gardens of the Zoological Society,

with notices respecting them, and a plan of the gardens, showing the buildings and enclosures in which animals are kept', *Hume Tracts*, 1 July 1831.

4 OSTRICH *À LA MODE*

1 Amanda Foreman, *Georgiana, Duchess of Devonshire* (London, 1998).
2 Arthur Trevenning Harris, 'Nitwits in Feathers', *The Saturday Evening Post* (24 December 1949), vol. CCXXII, p. 19.
3 Arthur Douglass, *Ostrich Farming in South Africa* (London, 1881); J. E. Duerden, 'Ostrich Farming in South Africa', *Journal of the Royal African Society*, XX (1920), pp. 19–24.
4 George Fen Manville, *Diamond Dyke, the Lone Farm on the Veldt: Story of a South African Adventure* (London, 1895).
5 Rob Nixon, 'The Feather Palace', *Transition*, LXXVII (1998), pp. 70–85; Rob Nixon, *Dream Birds: The Strange History of the Ostrich in Fashion, Food, and Fortune* (New York, 2000).
6 Sarah Abrevya Stein, *Plumes: Ostrich Feathers, Jews and a Lost World of Global Commerce* (New Haven, CT, 2008).
7 Sarah Abrevya Stein, '"Falling in Feathers": Jews and the Trans-Atlantic Ostrich Feather Trade', *The Journal of Modern History*, LXXIX (2007), pp. 772–812.
8 'Ostrich Feathers', *Scientific American*, VII/46 (1852), p. 362.
9 R. J. Moore-Colyer, 'Feathered Women and Persecuted Birds: The Struggle Against the Plumage Trade, *c.* 1860–1922', *Rural History*, XI (2000), pp. 57–73.
10 Duerden, 'Ostrich Farming in South Africa'.
11 Nixon, *Dream Birds*; Stein, *Plumes*; Thor Hansen, *Feathers* (New York, 2000).
12 Hansen, *Feathers*.
13 Stein, *Plumes*.
14 Thomas Rick, *Images of America: South Pasadena's Ostrich Farm* (Mount Pleasant, SC, 2007).

1 Linda Parker, *The San of Africa* (Minneapolis, MN, 2005).
2 British Museum, London, UK. Print by J. Carwitham (1741).
  Reg. No. 1914,0520.484.
3 Historia Augusta, *The Life of Commodus* (Cambridge, MA, 1921).
4 R. Lee, *Little Nellie's Bird-cage* (New York, 1885).
5 Rob Nixon, *Dream Birds: The Strange History of the Ostrich in Fashion, Food, and Fortune* (New York, 2000).
6 M. M. Shanawany and John Dingle, 'Ostrich Production Systems', FAO Animal Production and Health Paper 144, Rome (1999).
7 'Global Poultry Trends – Global Turkey Meat Consumption Flat', 27 October 2010, at www.thepoultrysite.com, accessed 27 April 2012.
8 S. Glozar Adabi et al., 'Egg Yolk Fatty Acid Profile of Avian Species – Influence on Human Nutrition', *Journal of Animal Physiology and Animal Nutrition* (October 2011), published online at http://onlinelibrary.wiley.com.
9 Pliny the Elder, *The Natural History*, Book 10.
10 Georges, Baron Cuvier, *The Class Aves* (London, 1829), vol. III.
11 Uma Devi Palanisamy et al., 'An Effective Ostrich Oil Bleaching Technique Using Peroxide Value as an Indicator', *Molecules*, XVI (2011), pp. 5,709–19.
12 Herodotus, *The Histories*, Book 4, chapters 168–99.
13 Cuvier, *The Class Aves*.
14 Ross G. Cooper, 'Ostrich (*Struthio camelus var. domesticus*) Skin and Leather: A Review Focused on Southern Africa', *World Poultry Science Journal*, LXII (2001), pp. 157–78.
15 Nixon, *Dream Birds*.
16 Cooper, 'Ostrich (*Struthio camelus var. domesticus*) Skin and Leather'.
17 Ibid.
18 Charles Mather and Amy Marshall, 'Living with Disease? Bioversity and Avian Influenza in Ostriches', *Agriculture and Human Values*, XXVIII (2011), pp. 153–65.
19 Ibid.

20 Sakchai Ruenphet et al., 'Strategies of Newcastle Disease Vaccination for Commercial Ostrich Farms in Japan', *The Journal of Veterinary Medical Science*, LXXIV (2012), pp. 905–8.

21 Shanawany and Dingle, 'Ostrich Production Systems'.

22 C. A. Madeiros, 'Use of Rabbits in Ostrich Farming', *The Veterinary Record*, 140 (1997), p. 668.

23 D. C. Bennett, A. Kaneko and Y. Karasawa, 'Maintenance Nitrogen Requirements of Adult Female Ostrichs (*Struthio camelus*)', *Journal of Animal Physiology and Animal Nutrition*, XCVI (2011), pp. 600–09.

24 Shanawany and Dingle, 'Ostrich Production Systems'.

6 OSTRICH SYMBOLISM AND IMAGERY

1 Chun Xue Wang et al., 'Archaeological Study of Ostrich Eggshell Beads Collected from SDG site', *Chinese Science Bulletin*, 54 (2009), pp. 3,887–95.

2 J. Tomczyk et al., 'Anthropological Analysis of the Osteological Material from an Ancient Tomb (Early Bronze Age) from the Middle Euphrates Valley, Terqa (Syria)', *International Journal of Osteoarchaeology*, XXI (2011), pp. 435–45.

3 W. H. Williams, ed., *Skelton: A Selection from the Poetical Works of John Skelton* (London, 1902).

4 Thomas Birch, *Memoirs of the Reign of Queen Elizabeth: From the Year 1581 Till Her Death* (London, 1754), vol. II.

5 C. G. Harlow, 'Shakespeare, Nashe, and the Ostridge Crux in *1 Henry IV*', *Shakespeare Quarterly*, XVII (1966), pp. 171–4.

6 R. Dodsley, *Select Fables of Esop and other Fabulists* (London, 1765).

7 See *The Concise Oxford Dictionary of Quotations*, 2nd edn (Oxford, 1981). The quotation was first published in a review of Dryden by Macaulay in the *Edinburgh Review* (January 1828).

8 David Chandler, 'Coleridge the Ostrich and Capell's Shakespeare', *Notes and Queries*, XLV (1980), pp. 192–3.

9 H. Chichester Hart, 'Suspending Ostrich Eggs in Churches', *Notes and Queries*, s8-v127 (1894), pp. 511–12.

10 J.T.F., 'Suspending Ostrich Eggs in Churches', *Notes and Queries*, s8-v127 (1894), pp. 434–5.

11 Claire Tomalin, *Charles Dickens: A Life* (London, 2011).

12 'The Surprising Strength of the Ostrich', *London Magazine*, 28 (1759), pp. 141–2.

13 *The Golden ABC* (London, 1840), p. 5.

14 Elwyn Jenkins, 'How Ostriches Ruled the Roost in Early Children's Books Set in South Africa', *English in Africa*, XXVI (1999), pp. 17–32.

15 *The Golden ABC*.

16 *Oxford Dictionary of National Biography* (Oxford, 2011).

17 Ibid.

18 Board of Trade Wreck Report for 'Benbow' and 'Ostrich' (1878).

Select Bibliography

Brown, Leslie H., *The Birds of Africa: Ostriches and Birds of Prey* (Princeton, NJ, 1986)

Cramp, Stanley, and K.E.L. Simmons, eds, *Handbook of the Birds of Europe, the Middle East and North Africa: The Birds of the Western Palearctic*, vol. 1: *Ostrich to Ducks* (Oxford, 1978)

Cromwright Schreiner, S. C., 'The Ostrich', *The Zoologist* (March 1897)

Deeming, D. Charles, ed., *The Ostrich: Biology, Production and Health* (Oxford, 1999)

Doughty, Robin W., *Feather Fashions and Bird Preservation: A Study in Nature Protection* (Berkeley, CA, 1975)

Drenowatz, Claire, and Charlie Eirod, eds, *The Ratite Encyclopaedia: Ostrich, Emu, Rhea* (San Antonio, TX, 1995)

Gallagher, Bill, Pauline Henderson and Danelle Coulson, *The South African Ostrich Cookbook* (Cape Town, 2000)

Laufer, Berthold, *Ostrich Egg-shell Cups of Mesopotamia and the Ostrich in Ancient and Modern Times* (Chicago, 1926)

Manville, George Fen, *Diamond Dyke, the Lone Farm on the Veldt: Story of a South African Adventure* (London, 1895)

Martin, Annie, *Home Life on an Ostrich Farm* (New York, 1891)

Nixon, Rob, *Dreambirds: The Strange History of the Ostrich in Fashion, Food, and Fortune* (New York, 1999)

Stein, Sarah Abrevya, *Plumes: Ostrich Feathers, Jews and a Lost World of Global Commerce* (New Haven, CT, 2008)

Wagner, Phillip, *The Ostrich Story: The Ostriches of Oudtshoorn* (Hong Kong, 1986)

Associations and Websites

AMERICAN OSTRICH ASSOCIATION
www.ostriches.org

BRITISH DOMESTICATED OSTRICH ASSOCIATION
www.ostrich.org.uk

CANADIAN OSTRICH ASSOCIATION
www.ostrich.ca

KLEIN KAROO INTERNATIONAL
www.kleinkaroo.com
Ostrich products

C. P. NEL MUSEUM, OUDTSHOORN
www.places.co.za/html/cpnel.html
Museum of the history of the ostrich industry

OSTRICH FARMING FOR A PROFIT
www.ostrichfarming.org

OSTRICH TOURISM
www.ostrichsa.co.za

SAHARA CONSERVATION FUND
www.saharaconservation.org/Ostrich
Preservation of the ostrich in West Africa

WORLD OSTRICH ASSOCIATION
www.world-ostrich.org

Acknowledgements

I would like to thank my family for their support while writing this book and for their help and encouragement during my pursuit of all things struthious. The great joy of writing *Ostrich* has been the hours spent researching the world's digital archives, a solo task, so all views expressed in this book are my own. Another great joy has been to observe the ostrich close-up and see at first hand what special birds they are.

I would like to thank Carol Moen Wing and Gerald Wing for their superb ostrich photographs. I owe a great deal of thanks to the production team at Reaktion Books who managed to turn a simple manuscript into the book you now have in your hands.

Photo Acknowledgements

The author and publishers wish to express their thanks to the below sources of illustrative material and/or permission to reproduce it. (Some sources uncredited in the captions for reasons of brevity are also given below.)

Photo Aberdeen University Library: p. 70; from Eleazar Albin, *A Supplement to the Natural History of Birds* . . . (London, 1740): p. 79; photo art.co.uk: p. 23; courtesy the author: pp. 8, 28, 30, 36, 37, 42, 50, 110, 111; photo Dan Barba/Stock Connection/Rex Features: p. 34; from Pierre Belon du Mans, *L'Histoire de la nature des oiseaux* . . . (Paris, 1555): p. 78; Bibliothèque de l'Institut de France, Paris: p. 35; British Museum, London (photos © Trustees of the British Museum): pp. 60, 63, 65, 66, 68, 72, 86, 89, 90, 93, 133, 142 (top), 152; photo Peter Brooker/Rex Features: p. 147; from George Buffon, *Histoire naturelle* . . . (Paris, 1801): p. 80; photo © Charles Plante Fine Arts/Bridgeman Art Library: p. 155; photos Corbis: pp. 24, 43, 49, 145; from W. Cornwallis Harris, *Portraits of the Game and Wild Animals of Southern Africa* . . . (London, 1840): p. 84; photo Creativ Studio Heinemann/WestEnd61/Rex Features: p. 38; photo John Curtis/Rex Features: p. 117; from William Daniell, *Interesting Selections from Animated Nature* . . . , vol. I (London, 1809): p. 81; photo Eye Ubiquitous/Rex Features: p. 57; photo F1 Online/Rex Features: p. 41; from Leopold Joseph Fitzinger, *Bilder-Atlas* . . . (Vienna, 1864): p. 82; photo Gallo Images/Rex Features: p. 26; from Conrad Gessner, *Icones animalium quadrupedum viviparorum* . . . , vol. II (Zurich, 1560): p. 73; photo Tony Heald/Nature Picture Library/Rex Features: p. 162; photo

Index